Tarot

Unlock the Power of Tarot Spreads and Learn About Psychic Tarot Card Reading, Symbolism, and Developing Your Intuition

© Copyright 2021

The contents of this book may not be reproduced, duplicated or transmitted without direct written permission from the author.

Under no circumstances will any legal responsibility or blame be held against the publisher for any reparation, damages, or monetary loss due to the information herein, either directly or indirectly.

Legal Notice:

This book is copyright protected. This is only for personal use. You cannot amend, distribute, sell, use, quote or paraphrase any part or the content within this book without the consent of the author.

Disclaimer Notice:

Please note the information contained within this document is for educational and entertainment purposes only. Every attempt has been made to provide accurate, up to date and reliable complete information. No warranties of any kind are expressed or implied. Readers acknowledge that the author is not engaging in the rendering of legal, financial, medical or professional advice. The content of this book has been derived from various sources. Please consult a licensed professional before attempting any techniques outlined in this book.

By reading this document, the reader agrees that under no circumstances is the author responsible for any losses, direct or indirect, which are incurred as a result of the use of information contained within this document, including, but not limited to, errors, omissions, or inaccuracies.

Your Free Gift (only available for a limited time)

Thanks for getting this book! If you want to learn more about various spirituality topics, then join Mari Silva's community and get a free guided meditation MP3 for awakening your third eye. This guided meditation mp3 is designed to open and strengthen ones third eye so you can experience a higher state of consciousness. Simply visit the link below the image to get started.

https://spiritualityspot.com/meditation

Contents

INTRODUCTION 1
CHAPTER ONE: HOW TO READ THE CARDS 3
    The Root of the Meaning 3
    Tarot Card Instructions 4
    Selecting the Deck 4
    Modern or Traditional? 6
    4 Ways to Shuffle Tarot Cards 9
    Tarot Card Spreads 10
    How to Interpret Reversed Cards 14
CHAPTER TWO: DEVELOPING INTUITION 15
    Developing Intuition 16
CHAPTER THREE: THE MAJOR ARCANA 20
CHAPTER FOUR: THE FOOL'S JOURNEY 24
    Upright 24
    Understanding the Fool's Journey 27
CHAPTER FIVE: MAJOR CARDS 1 - 11 28
    The Magician 28
    The High Priestess 31
    The Empress 34
    The Emperor 38

THE HIEROPHANT	42
THE LOVERS	45
THE CHARIOT	50
THE STRENGTH	52
THE HERMIT	55
THE WHEEL OF FORTUNE	57
THE JUSTICE	60
CHAPTER SIX: CARDS 12 – 21	**63**
THE HANGED MAN	63
THE DEATH	66
THE TEMPERANCE	69
THE DEVIL	71
THE TOWER	74
THE JUDGMENT	78
THE WORLD	80
CHAPTER SEVEN: THE MINOR ARCANA	**83**
CHAPTER EIGHT: WANDS OF FIRE	**85**
THE CARDS	86
CHAPTER NINE: SWORDS OF AIR	**91**
CHAPTER TEN: PENTACLES OF EARTH	**98**
CHAPTER ELEVEN: CUPS OF WATER	**102**
CHAPTER TWELVE: TIPS TO DEEPEN YOUR UNDERSTANDING OF TAROT SYMBOLISM	**109**
CONCLUSION	**111**
HERE'S ANOTHER BOOK BY MARI SILVA THAT YOU MIGHT LIKE	**112**
YOUR FREE GIFT (ONLY AVAILABLE FOR A LIMITED TIME)	**113**
REFERENCES	**114**

Introduction

Did you ever stop and think what it would be like if you could interpret every message the Universe has for you? Have you ever wondered if you could see into your future? If you have, then you are in the right place. Most people struggle to learn more about themselves. They may want to learn about their past, present, or future to gain a better understanding of why life is full of the various challenges that we all face. Some also want to learn more about the dangers they may encounter to prevent them. They may also want to see what happened in their past that made them behave the way they do now.

This book will help you understand yourself better. You can finally map your thoughts and emotions back to an event or situation in your life. Few people believe that a simple set of cards can do this, but do you? Even if you don't, I'm positive you will after reading this book. Whether you are a beginner or just want to refresh your memory, this is the perfect book for you.

A lot goes into tarot cards and tarot reading. This book explains the basics, and it will help you learn more about yourself through Tarot reading. The Universe has a message for everybody. You need only to be strong enough to listen to the message and interpret it. Many people have used Tarot cards to understand these messages. If you are curious to learn more about Tarot cards and their meanings, you are in the right place. This book helps you with a program paced and easy to understand.

This book looks at the basics of Tarot and introduces layouts and other important information you need if you wish to read the cards. The first chapter covers information about how you should select the right deck and the different spreads you can use. The latter chapters of the book cover the different cards found in the deck of cards. The book also covers tips and information to read tarot cards. You must adhere to these instructions so your reading is accurate. The different cards found in the Tarot deck and their interpretation has also been in the book. You can predict the future or identify a person's past using these interpretations.

There are different layouts used for a tarot reading. The three layouts most commonly used have been described. The different positions in the layout are also explained to help you identify a person's past, present, or future. To better show you how a reading works, the book also includes a sample reading to help you determine the steps you need to follow. You also learn more about the different types of cards found in a Tarot deck. We will also focus on specific cards from the Minor and Major Arcana since those are extremely important for you during a reading.

Chapter One: How to Read the Cards

Most people are wary about receiving any messages from the Universe. There are important signs and messages that the Universe leaves for you, so you must be open to receiving these messages. You can use Tarot cards to help you decipher this meaning. Each card in the deck has a different meaning because of the cards' images and the connections between them.

The Root of the Meaning

Experts believe that the meaning behind Tarot cards come from within us. Your subconscious mind helps you decipher the meaning of every card since your subconscious mind understands various aspects of your life and hence is known as your inner guide. Most people ignore their subconscious mind because they fear what the future may hold for you—the subconscious guides you to reach for any card in the deck. Since most people only rely on their conscious mind, they ignore the subconscious mind and its signals. It is only when you let your mind lead you that you find meaning when you use tarot cards.

Tarot Card Instructions

This section leaves you with instructions and tips to use when you read cards. Your understanding of tarot cards will improve when you use them. As they say, "Practice makes perfect." The instructions in this chapter and other information in the book will help you improve. Before you begin reading, you must know what the objective of your tarot reading is.

1. Before you begin the Tarot reading, before you begin to understand how to read the cards, you have to familiarize yourself with the cards. Look at the images and see if you can find any connection. Try reading on yourself before you conduct a reading for another person.

2. Study what each means and also how they can be interpreted. It is easier if you can put a meaning to the cards in the deck. It is better to know the meaning of each before you conduct a tarot reading.

Selecting the Deck

The most important thing to consider with Tarot reading is the deck. If you do not have the right deck with you, then your reading will not have the correct outcome. Every Tarot card has its own energy and meaning, so you need to make sure you choose the right deck, especially the one you connect with.

Choose a Deck You Connect With

This is the most important thing to remember. You must always choose a card you intuitively and personally connect with. You may have people around you who talk about the Rider-Waite deck, the Wild Unknown deck, or any other deck. This does not mean you should choose a deck only because someone told you about them. You can always try different decks and see which one works best for you. There may be decks that cause you to break into a sweat. This means the deck is not right for you.

If you are in love with a specific deck, use that first. If you live close to a bookstore or new age store, go to the Tarot section and pick up a deck. Play around with them. See what energy you feel when you choose a deck. Do you feel a connection, either intuitive or personal, when you hold the deck in your hand? If you want to purchase a deck online, you can always look for them on Google. Go through the images in every deck and see if a connection. Always stick to your intuition.

Understand the Imagery

Look at the cards in every deck you choose and go through every one of them. If you are looking at the deck online, look at as many images as you can on any social media platform. You can use the hashtag #fountaintarot to look for them on social media. There are numerous hashtags you can use for the same.

When you look at the images, analyze how you react to the image on the card. Do you like the patterns and colors? Do you find other decks or images more attractive? For instance, someone may prefer the Fairy deck because of the bright colors and images. Others prefer the Radiant Rider-Waite deck because of the bright colors used in the images.

Also, look at every card and get a sense of what each means to you. You must look at both the Minor and Major Arcana cards. Some decks do not have a story or imagery on the Minor Arcana cards. This does not help you choose the right deck online since you cannot view all the cards in the deck. If you choose such a deck, you should go to the store and buy them.

Know Your Level

Most beginners prefer to use popular Tarot decks since they are easy to understand. One such example is the Rider-Waite deck. This deck's imagery is easy to understand. The images are practical and straightforward. Since this is a popular deck, there is a lot of information available on the Internet to help you understand how to use the deck better. You can also choose a deck with minimalist and clear imagery to help you connect better with the symbols. If you are an experienced reader or want to look at a complex deck, choose a different tarot deck. One such example is the Thoth Tarot deck. This deck of cards is known for its depth and complexity. You can also use other abstract decks.

You need not limit yourself to a simple or popular deck if you are new to Tarot. You can always choose the deck you connect with, both personally and intuitively.

Modern or Traditional?

Have you always thought of using traditional or old Tarot decks? If yes, you can choose different decks, such as the Original Rider Waite Tarot deck, Visconti Tarot deck, or Tarot de Marseilles deck. If you are drawn to more modern Tarot decks, pick whichever one feels right for you. The new Tarot decks that are coming now are brilliant. The imagery relates to the current times and has beautiful artwork. Did you know you could also create your very own deck using different imagery and artwork? You can have a knight roaming the streets or even have a beautiful cup designed for the deck.

Read "The Little White Book"

Tarot decks often come with their own books that explain the imagery and artwork used on the cards. Some decks come with more information when compared to other decks. Some decks have minimal or no information. To know what every card in the Tarot deck means, you must read the Little White Book that comes with every Tarot deck. This book will usually give you all the information you need about the different cards in the deck. If the book that comes with the deck does not have enough information, you can always check if there is any information about that deck on the Internet. You can let your intuition help you determine the meaning behind every card in the deck. If you can do this, you can understand every card in the deck without a book.

Choose the Right Fit

Every Tarot deck comes in different sizes. Always choose the right size for your reading sessions. You can use tarot decks when you read at parties or for small groups. To use the deck for personal readings, you should choose a face-to-face client reading. You can also read them on the go if you use the mini tarot cards.

The size of the deck is important, especially for shuffling and handling the cards. If they are too small or big, it may become difficult for both you and the clients to handle. So, use the cards, practice with them, and learn to handle them before you perform any reading.

Determine the Objective

Always determine what the objective of your tarot readings is. You also need to know how you want to connect with them. Do you want to find love? Are you looking for peace and quiet? Choose the Tarot deck basis for your objective. The best thing about Tarot decks is that you can choose from different backgrounds. Since you have multiple options, you can choose the one that fits your desires and needs. If you are a professional, you must choose from different decks best suited for you and your situation.

Shuffling the Deck

Every reading starts here. You need to shuffle them well, but few people know how to do this. This is one of the most fundamental aspects of card reading, but they often go unmentioned. There are different tricky elements to a Tarot reading, and if you do not perform aspects of Tarot cards correctly, the reading will be incorrect. This deck is one of the most important aspects that need close attention.

This section covers techniques to help you shuffle your deck correctly, but before we look at these techniques, let us focus on why you need to shuffle these cards. If you look at it simply, you bond with them and images when you shuffle the deck. You and the cards begin to share the same energy. When you handle the cards well, you step into the same energy space as the cards. This is when you begin conversing with them.

When you shuffle cards, you give yourself enough time to focus on the topic or question. This helps you interact emotionally, physically, and spiritually with the deck. Experts recommend you use this time to begin your readings since you are shifting from the usual mindset into the world of tarot reading. This is a powerful and simple ritual that will help you do the same.

Now, let us look at the different techniques. Understand that there is no right or wrong way to shuffle the tarot deck. You can shuffle them in any way you want. Each tarot reader has his/her own way to shuffle the cards, and you may come across different methods. If you go to a Tarot reading event, you will come across different styles. Some may pile them, while others may rearrange the cards gently. You may come across some readers who bang the cards to shuffle them.

You can work with the approaches mentioned in this section and invent a style for yourself. When you begin Tarot reading, you will know which method works best for you. Do not worry if you feel awkward when you read Tarot cards. Since the cards in a Tarot deck are larger than a regular deck of cards, it takes time for one to handle them with ease.

Some suggest that you are disrespecting them if you do not handle them well, but this is not true since we all forge a different relationship with the cards in our decks. If you perform a tarot reading with bad intentions, you are disrespectful. If you approach Tarot reading with a good attitude, it does not matter if you drop them on the floor. Let us now learn how you can shuffle Tarot cards.

4 Ways to Shuffle Tarot Cards

The Classic Shuffle

This is the simplest shuffle. You need only to divide the deck into two piles and shift the piles to make sure the cards interweave. You can use a bridge shuffle to try a fancy shuffle. You may take time to get the hang of this when you use tarot cards, but this is one of the easiest and fastest ways to shuffle the deck.

Regrouping and Spreading

This is an evocative method. Spread them on the table, so it looks good to you. You can stick to a pattern based on aesthetics. So, get fancy with the spread. When you regroup the cards, try using a different pattern to pick them up.

Pile the Cards

Divide them into smaller piles. Group them in a different order. You can either shuffle the pairs and then pile them together or shuffle the deck when it is integrated.

Shuffle in Your Hands

This is a very simple method. You split the deck of cards in your hand and place them in different stops in the deck. This may be difficult to do when you start tarot reading. The process but is a great way to get in the zone. This is a meditative and comforting technique to handle all the cards in the deck before you read them.

Tarot Card Spreads

Most people do not know how to choose the spread that works for them. There are many spreads to choose from, and you can work with them all before choosing the one that works for you. This section covers simple tarot card spreads you can use when you start off with tarot card reading. There are other spreads you can use, but those are often complicated to use. The spreads covered in this section can be used by a beginner easily.

The three-card spread is one of the most commonly used spreads, and this is one that most beginners use for their first reading. The other common spread is the five-card and Celtic cross spread. You can choose any of these spreads, depending on your convenience. These spreads help you answer all your questions. Some spreads may use only one card from the deck, while others may use the entire deck.

Every spread has its characteristics and attributes, and these give the spreads their power. Some Tarot spreads are standardized, while tarot readers can develop other spreads. You can develop your own Tarot spread depending on your style and requirement. You can base these layouts on certain adjustments you may want to make to the layout. This section does not cover every spread but covers the most important and common ones.

There are many spreads used for a tarot reading. Of those, the three-card spread, five-card spread, and Celtic-cross spread are the most famous.

The Three-Card Spread

The three-card spread is the easiest spread for a Tarot reading, especially if you are a beginner. You can use this spread to gain an insight into the present, past, and future. You cannot use a Tarot reading to predict what may happen in the future, but reading can help you determine what or how you may feel in the future. First, work on the three-card spread before you work on the other two spreads mentioned in this section.

Draw three cards from the deck and spread them in the following manner:

☐ ☐ ☐

The card in the center will tell you about yourself or the person you are performing the reading for. The card will tell you how you are feeling about yourself. You can use the card on the left to learn more about the different obstacles and opportunities that come your way, while the one on your right helps you determine the solution.

Celtic Cross Spread

This is one of the most popular spreads used by both beginners and experts. The layout is straightforward, but it holds great energy and power. Since there is strong energy around this spread, people have used it to answer numerous questions. Many secret societies also use this spread to answer different questions about their life.

Cross/Circle   *Staff*

There are two parts to the Celtic cross - the circle or cross and the staff. The former has six cards, while the latter has four cards. The circle or cross resembles the Celtic cross found in Ireland. The cross in Ireland has many spokes placed perpendicular to each other. These spokes are linked using a circle. This symbol is a connection between the matter of all events and beings at a certain time and the spirit. It is believed that the energy within the spokes is feminine and works with the masculine energy present in the staff. The Celtic cross spread is a representation of the duality of nature. This spread and energy represent the polarity of the human psyche.

The circle or cross-section of the spread has two crosses. The smaller cross is at the center of the spread. There are two cards that make the cross in the center. The bigger cross has six cards, including the small cross in the center. The larger cross helps you identify and understand various events that have occurred in the past and those that may occur in the future. The card on the left of the cross depicts the past, while the one on the right depicts the future. The cards at the top and bottom of the cross depict the conscious and subconscious minds, respectively.

The cards in the Staff section of the spread describe your life. These rarely relate to the present. You need to let your intuition guide you in interpreting the spread. You can understand your future better and also help people understand their future better.

Five-Card Spread

The three-card spread helps you obtain a lot of information, but the five-card spread helps you dive into the question's details. You can use either the three-card or five-card spread to find the root cause of any problem. You can spread the five-card spread in the form of a cross. It is often structured in this way. The base of the five-card spread is the three-card spread. In this spread, three cards will relate to the past, present, and future in the center of the cross.

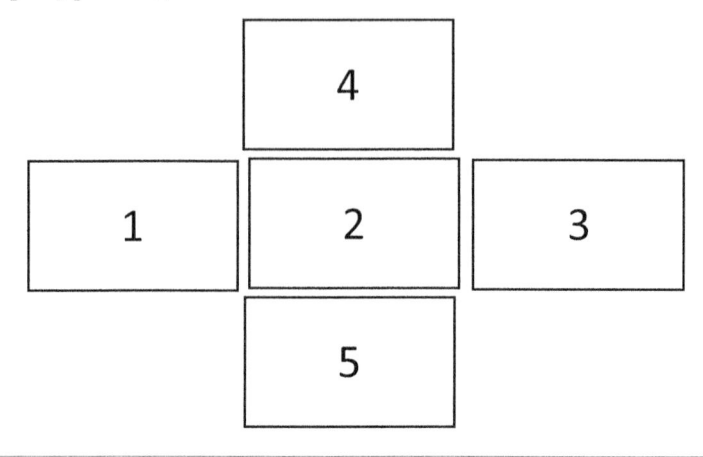

```
          +-----+
          |  4  |
          +-----+
   +---+  +-----+  +---+
   | 1 |  |  2  |  | 3 |
   +---+  +-----+  +---+
          +-----+
          |  5  |
          +-----+
```

1. Past
2. Present
3. Future
4. Core reason for circumstances
5. Potential of situation

The cards may not represent the actual outcome, but they will show you the brightest and darkest situations and outcomes hidden in the current situation.

You can also use a rectangular formation when you use the five-card spread. You can use this formation to explore various situations and themes. The spread makes it easy to look at different variations. When you use the rectangular formation, the theme or the main card is placed between the other four cards. You need to pull the theme card last.

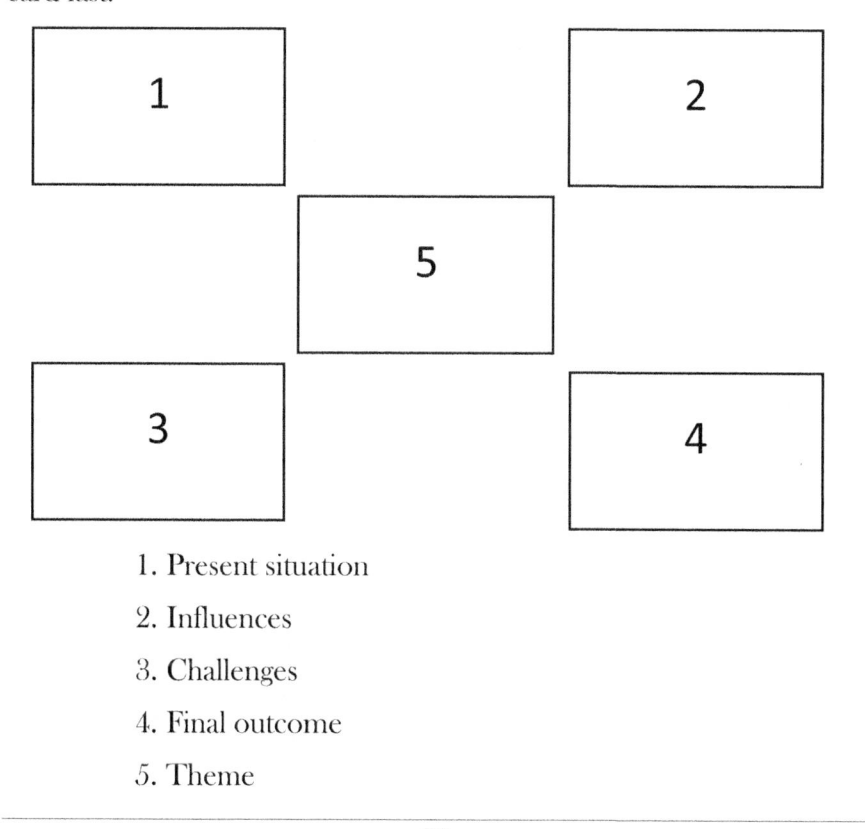

```
┌─────────┐            ┌─────────┐
│    1    │            │    2    │
└─────────┘            └─────────┘
        ┌─────────┐
        │    5    │
        └─────────┘
┌─────────┐            ┌─────────┐
│    3    │            │    4    │
└─────────┘            └─────────┘
```

1. Present situation
2. Influences
3. Challenges
4. Final outcome
5. Theme

Some readers prefer using the other four cards in the formation to understand the theme. They make loose interpretations of these cards when they pull them out of the deck, but you can choose what each position should represent. For example, these cards can represent your conflicts, fears, desires, and another's perspective or any lesson you may need to learn.

How to Interpret Reversed Cards

When you obtain a reversed card in your reading, it can be interpreted in different ways. It is for this reason a reversed card is extremely important to read carefully. A reversed card can be interpreted in multidimensional ways. Only when you do this can you understand or answer any questions you may have about your life. A reversed card holds as much importance as an upright card in a tarot reading, and you can make the right decisions based on the reading of these cards. You need to consider these components of reversed cards before you read or interpret them:

    1. Understand the meaning and interpretation of a reversed card. The later chapters in the book talk about how to interpret the different cards in the tarot deck.

    2. Understand how you should interpret the card when it is in the upright position

    3. Look for ways to determine the increase and decrease in energy levels of the card

    4. Learn to combine the meaning of upright and reversed cards during a reading

    5. Is there any energy blocked or repressed in the reversed card?

It is easier to use your previous experience to determine how you should interpret the card.

Chapter Two: Developing Intuition

Have you ever gone to a reading where the person reading the cards for you does not know what to say? You wonder if they have forgotten what the card means. This frustrates you because you went there to understand something about yourself, and the lack of information frustrates you. This can happen to you, as well. Here is where you may want to open the Little White Book and read everything about the card, including its meaning. Does this help you, though? Will your reading help the person?

Sure, you can use your book to help you understand the cards, but are you sure the meaning and symbolism are accurate? This need not be the case. You may feel doubt on numerous occasions if you do not develop your intuition. You may feel one thing when you look at the card, but the book you are using will tell you something else.

What should you do here? How will you correctly identify the meaning of the tarot card? Never ignore your intuition since this is the key to understanding every card's meaning in the deck you use. Interpret the meaning of the cards in the deck with confidence and ease. This chapter will look at how to understand the meaning of a tarot card using your intuition. We will also look at steps you can use to improve your intuition. Intuitive tarot reading is the best way to perform a reading since you are not trying to force the card's meaning from the white book into your reading. The book's meaning can have a different meaning, and you may interpret the imagery and symbolism differently.

Developing Intuition

One of the best ways to develop your intuition is through meditation. Through meditation, you can delve deeper into the symbolism and meaning every tarot card offers. You can go around your conscious mind and focus on the message the card has for you. This helps you connect with your intuition. When you learn to relax your mind, you learn to control your thought process. You open up the path towards your subconscious mind, making it easier for you to tap into your intuition. You learn to let your intuition tell you what to make of the tarot card in front of you. In this process, you need to relax your body and mind. This is the only way you can understand the imagery and symbolism of the Tarot card you have chosen.

Choose the Card

When you use this technique, you learn more about the tarot card. This helps you improve your intuition. Shuffle the deck and choose any card from the deck. If you have a specific card in mind, place it in front of you. You can use a card based on a specific situation or event in your life. For instance, to invite love into life, select the Lovers card. You can also choose the Two Cups card.

Set the Ambiance

You need to choose the place and time when you want to work on developing your intuition. Choose a spot and time when you know you will not be disturbed. Be comfortable and disconnect from the world. Get rid of any distractions. If you want it to be completely quiet, you can wear earbuds. Alternatively, you can listen to a meditation CD if it helps you concentrate. You can also dim the lights and burn incense sticks. Sit straight because lying down will only make you sleepy. Place the tarot card you have selected before you.

Focus on Your Breath

When you find yourself in a comfortable position, focus on your breath. Breathe normally and only through your nose. When you breathe in, observe what you feel when you breathe in. How do you feel when the air passes through your nostrils? Continue to breathe normally and focus on the sensation of the air on your breath. If you find thoughts flitting through your mind, observe them, and then let go of them. Think of them as clouds floating away. When you manage to do this, you should go back to focusing on your breath.

Relax

Now, focus on your body. Take a deep breath and let the air enter your body. Feel every molecule in the air you have breathed in; fill every inch of your body with energy. When you breathe out, imagine every muscle and cell in your body relaxing. Move your focus to your head, eyes, shoulders, neck, arms, chest, back, hips, legs, and toes. Let your body relax. When you feel like you are floating, you will be at peace.

Focus on the Card

Place the tarot card you have selected in front of you and focus on it. Do not glare at the card but look at it with a soft gaze. Take two or three deep breaths. If you find thoughts entering your mind, do not give them any importance. You should observe them and think of them floating away like clouds. Focus on your breath and look at the tarot card in front of you.

Now focus on the card and imagine that the figures are growing larger in front of you. Imagine that the figures and images are becoming life-size. Now, imagine yourself stepping into the imagery in the card. Look at your surroundings and observe what you see. Ask yourself who is with you on the card. Make a note of the colors and objects that stand out.

Walk towards an object you connect within the card and touch it. Feel the texture and observe what you feel and hear. Smell the air around you. If you find something you can eat, walk towards that object and taste it. Once you have done this, imagine you are a figure in the card. Become this person on the card. How do you feel about being this figure? How do you think or feel when you are this person? What is your attitude towards your circumstances as this person? Now talk to yourself in the same way you think the character would talk to you. What do you want to tell yourself? What message or advice do you want to give?

Look at your surroundings one more time. Is there something that makes you happy? Does one specific area or object in the surroundings give you energy? Does anything in the imagery concern you? Are you anxious about something in the imagery? Can you notice the areas in your body that feel the tension and anxiety? Is it possible for you to release that nervous energy?

Look at the various symbols and objects on the card. How can you use them? Is there a symbolic meaning for the objects you have picked up? Why do you think the objects and symbols are around you? Pay attention to your surroundings one last time and note what you did not find the last time you looked at the imagery. You are almost done, so step out of the figure in the card. Now, slowly step out of the card. Focus on the card until it reaches its size.

Awaken

You must acknowledge all the work you have completed until the moment. You should also know that you could always go back to your zone of peace and quiet whenever you want. Slowly bring your focus to your surroundings. Take a few deep breaths and feel the surrounding energy fill your feet, belly, hands, and your entire body. If you have closed your eyes, slowly open them. You will feel energized and refreshed.

Understand and Note Your Insights

When you are done with your meditation process, make a note of everything you saw. Also, write down your thoughts and emotions. Keep a separate journal to write these down.

Chapter Three: The Major Arcana

These cards are the most important cards in the deck. These cards represent various karmic influences, archetypal themes, and life lessons. These cards talk about those experiences that influence your journey. The cards in this Arcana are complex and deep in many ways. These cards are synonymous with human consciousness and tell you the stories and lessons passed through the years.

The Major Arcana includes 22 cards – one unnumbered and 21 numbered cards. These cards are called the Trump cards. The unnumbered card, known as The Fool, is an important part of the Major Arcana. The character is very important since he meets new teachers and learns various lessons on his journey. When he reaches the World card, he finally completes his journey. This journey is called the Fool's journey and is one of the best ways to understand Major Arcana's cards.

What Does a Card From this Arcana Mean?

When you look at a card from the Major Arcana during a Tarot reading session, you are being asked to reflect on various themes and lessons you are experiencing. The cards in this Arcana set the scene for the entire session since every other card you pick from the deck will relate to the Major arcana card.

Is it Okay to Have a Majority of Major Arcana Cards During a Reading?

If you pull out too many cards from the major arcana during a reading, it implies that you are going through some life-changing events, and these events will have a long-term effect. The cards indicate that you should pay attention to what is happening in your life so you can proceed further in your personal and spiritual quest. If any of the Arcana cards are reversed, it indicates you are not focusing on those aspects of your life, so first focus on them before you move forward.

There are 22 cards that fall under the major arcana. This section lists the names of these cards and how they can be interpreted for a reading.

- The Cards
- The Fool

This card shows you are spontaneous. It indicates that you face the world with your head held high, but you do not consider the problems and issues you may encounter in the process.

The Magician

The magician is an active card depicting your conscious awareness. This card states you are charismatic and have the willpower to take over any challenge that life throws at you.

High Priestess

The high priestess depicts your mysterious subconscious. This card indicates you have an inherent potential you have not realized. When you realize this potential, you can achieve whatever you want.

The Empress

This card indicates to you that you are attracted to an individual. It represents the natural and sensual aspects of the world. It is also called Juno, who is the Queen of all Roman gods. This card also represents feminine characteristics.

The Emperor

This card depicts the Father. It shows you are subjected to multiple rules in life. It also indicates that you do great under these conditions and finds a way to meet your goals and dreams.

The Hierophant

This card indicates you will meet with a spiritual advisor or mentor. You will connect with them and also grow on your spiritual journey.

The Lovers

This card can be interpreted as you being ready to enter a relationship. But this does not necessarily mean it will be a healthy relationship. You might have to work on the relationship to make it last.

The Chariot

The Chariot depicts your will power. It shows you have the power to achieve greatness and victory in your life.

Strength, Judgment, and Temperance

These cards indicate exactly what their name suggests. You will know how strong you are and also more about your morals.

Hermit

This card depicts that you are in search of knowledge, which could mean anything.

Wheel of Fortune

This card indicates that you will experience a change in life. Based on the different influences in your life, you can predict the changes you will have.

Hanged Man

This card shows you are a person who has sacrificed a lot in life. It also indicates this will continue.

Death

This card does not mean you are nearing death. It only implies there are certain habits or aspects of your personality you may have to change. It just means you will be moving on from a certain path of living into another.

Devil

This card will help you understand the different external factors affecting you, but you are ignorant of these external factors, so it is difficult for you to overcome your problems.

Tower

The card tells you that you will discover something new about yourself soon.

Star, Moon, and Sun

These cards talk about the effect of the astronomical bodies on your life. They depict the softness, calmness, and brightness of the sun, moon, and stars.

World

This card talks about your happiness. It tells you about whether you are happy with yourself and the surrounding environment. It helps you understand what you feel most content with.

Chapter Four: The Fool's Journey

Upright

Key Meaning or Interpretation

Freedom, new beginnings, travel, adventure, innocence, originality, carelessness, foolishness, travel, youth, idealism, lack of commitment, spontaneity

General Interpretation

This is the first card of the Major Arcana, and as mentioned above, it indicates new beginnings. If you pull this card during your reading, it means you may experience a new adventure soon. The adventure will take you on a path where you need to take a leap of faith. You will but learn from the experience and grow as an individual. Here, the new adventure can be anything – it can even mean you may move to a new country. You will welcome the change this card indicates to you. The Fool has a positive meaning, but it will take you a while to interpret the card's correct meaning when the card appears with other cards.

Romance

This card is both spontaneous and exciting, but it is a little ambiguous. If you are in a relationship, this card indicates that you are very excited about being in love and cannot contain your emotions. If another person is asking you whether they can be in a committed relationship, this card means the person is not ready to commit to a relationship. If you are single, this card can mean you will enter into a carefree and impulsive romance. If the card appears, be prepared for a beautiful and fun relationship. You should keep your eyes open so you do not miss true love.

Profession

If you have pulled this card out, it means the opportunity will come knocking on your door. You can take a leap of faith and start your business or start a new job. There may be people around you who do not know what you are doing or put you down but learn to be patient with them. Explain to them what you want to do, but do not let their words deter you. If you are working on projects at the moment, the card indicates that you will work on the project with renewed energy and fresh ideas. This card indicates there will be advancements in the project. Do your research and be extremely clever. Do not be afraid. Work hard on any new move or project.

Health

This card is a great indicator of physical health. If you are ill, the card indicates that you will regain your energy and strength. The card also indicates that you are prone to meeting with an accident, so you need to be extra careful. The card can also bring good news since it indicates pregnancy or the start of a new life.

Spirituality

This card indicates you are at the start of your new journey. You will learn more about your journey and see how you will move onto a new path. Since the card indicates renewed energy, you will be eager to try numerous approaches. There will be people who cannot understand your journey but always do what is best for you.

Reversed

Carelessness, recklessness, stupidity, apathy, irrationality, distraction, negligence, lack of hope, faith, or fun

General Interpretation

The meaning of the reversed card is the same as the upright card, a new beginning. When you reverse this card, it indicates that the new beginning may not be one you are keen to consider. The new beginning is coming your way. The reversed card indicates that you are behaving recklessly towards the people around you. The card can imply a lack of fun, hope, faith, and irrational thinking.

Romance

When reversed, this card indicates that your pursuit of adventure will hold you back from the love you want or need. It can also cause uncertainty and problems in any relationship. If this card is reversed, it could mean that your relationship may involve some excitement. This card implies that new issues and problems may crop up in your relationship.

Profession

When this card is reversed, it shows financial opportunities that can be promising. You need to exercise caution. You must do your homework before you ever commit to something new. You should never let the people around you take advantage of you. You may become restless in your position at work and probably want to start your own business. Think before you do anything. You should never let yourself be held back because of a lack of confidence. Never be afraid and know that your ideas are valid.

Health

When this card is reversed, it means you can try different means to resolve any issues you may have. If you have the reversed card in your reading, it means you are accident-prone, and you must know your surroundings.

Spiritual

When you look at the card in a spiritual context, the reversed card indicates that you are looking for a new experience. You want to get rid of your old habits and patterns. You may surprise people around you but do what pleases you.

Understanding the Fool's Journey

As mentioned earlier, the Fool's journey is only a metaphor. This card's journey is an indicator of your journey and the different phases you go through in life. The cards in the Major Arcana indicates the journey that the Fool will go through. Here are the steps that the Fool will go through in life:

- The Fool learns all his life lessons from the other cards in the Arcana.
- This card represents those people taking on a new adventure. It can also talk about people leaving home for the first time.
- The card also represents those graduating, moving to a new city, starting a new company or job, and others.
- The card represents those individuals who are excited and brave to take up anything that comes their way.
- This card indicates that the individual is on the path to finding oneself. It also indicates that the person is keen to incorporate all his learnings to overcome different situations.

As mentioned earlier, there are 22 cards in the major arcana. Each card represents an important life lesson that the Fool will learn. The Major Arcana cards represent experiences that every individual will go through at some point in his life. The next two chapters talk about the 22 cards in the Major Arcana and how they relate to an individual's experience.

Chapter Five: Major Cards 1 – 11

The Magician

Upright Position

Key Meanings

Influence, power, resourcefulness, willpower, ability, skill, intellect, psychic powers, logic, and concentration

General Interpretation

When this card appears in your reading, it means you have all the abilities and skills you need to succeed. The Universe will do whatever it can to align all the positive changes your way. This card shows you should use your concentration, willpower, and intellect to ensure what happens. When you pull this card out during your reading, it means you have the ability and power to achieve your goals. The card also refers to the people in your life who can help you achieve your goals. You can contact the people around you from whom you can learn.

Romance

This card indicates a positive outcome in your life. If you are in a relationship, this card means you will move to a deeper and new level in your relationship where you will commit to each other. If you are single, the card indicates that now is the best time for you to meet somebody. Your partner will always be serious about you and will treat you well.

Profession

With Profession, this card indicates that you will have new opportunities. This means you will need to be brave and use your original ideas to improve your skills. Do not tell people your ideas because it does not bode well to give away your secrets. The card indicates that you will be promoted. You will feel self-assured and powerful. You should remember that great things would come your way. This card signifies that you will be presented with new tasks and opportunities. You may get the chance to mentor someone or may even mentor someone else. The card indicates that your finances will improve soon, and you will make money due to new opportunities.

Health

Your good health and strength will come back if you feel drained or have been ill recently. If your health no longer improves, you may need to try new alternative therapies. This card indicates that you need to approach a powerful and experienced healer so you have the boost you need.

Spirituality

In terms of spirituality, this card indicates now is a great time for you to work on spiritual development. If you have always had an interest in the subject of spirituality, you can now concentrate on this area. This will help you manage spirituality and channel your magical energy easily. You will be surprised to see how you will benefit from this new learning if you learn to concentrate and channel your energy.

If you are interested in psychic development, this card indicates that you have latent abilities.

Reversed Position

Key Meaning or Interpretation

Greed, manipulation, trickery, untrustworthiness, conniving, unused ability, lack of mental clarity, and cunning

General Interpretation

When the reverse of this card appears in your reading, it indicates that you need to be careful about any opportunities. You should never let your doubt stop you from choosing or working on an opportunity. If the card refers to any person, it means this person is trying to manipulate or use you despite them being trustworthy and knowledgeable. Look out for greedy and deceitful people and always be careful about the people you trust.

Romance

If you are in a relationship, and this card has appeared in your life, it means you need to be more honest and open with your partner. To manipulate a situation to ensure you get whatever you want, you should never do that. It is best to use honesty to fulfill your needs and desires. This card also indicates that your partner may be selfish and mean, despite him or her appearing to be trustworthy. If you are single, this card suggests that you are becoming very cynical about your future life. You may feel like you will not attract the right people in your life. You should never lose faith. Remember to stay positive and always send light and love into the world.

Money and Career

If the reverse card appears in your reading, it indicates that you are not using your skills and abilities to the fullest. You must learn to make the best use of all the opportunities available to you. If you are experiencing self-doubt, find a way to overcome it and achieve your goals. Spend time to understand why you feel the way you do and determine what is holding you back. This card indicates that the people around you often hold you back from taking on a new adventure. If you find yourself stuck in a rut because of your finances, take the right approach and change your circumstances.

Health

This card is a positive card when it comes to health, regardless of whether it is in the upright or reversed position. It indicates that you should trust in your ability to heal, so you can kick start the process of healing. If you do suffer from any mental health issues, meet with a professional soon.

Spirituality

This card indicates that you should no longer follow your old spiritual path. It is important for you to explore a new path and remove the old beliefs you may have had about your spirituality. Try to get rid of any beliefs that hinder your ability to function or work. You can use different methods to discover your spirituality. God also indicates that you must only use your power and prowess for good.

The High Priestess

Upright Position

Key Meanings

Unattainability, desirability, mystery, spirituality, creativity, subconscious, thirst for knowledge, sensuality, fertility, higher power

General Interpretation

The card represents these characteristics:

- Common sense
- Intuition
- Sensuality
- Mystery

If this card appears in your reading, it indicates that you should now trust your gut feeling and behave in accordance with those feelings. Also, pay attention to various signs, symbols, and images that the Universe is sending your way, especially when you pick this card up during your reading.

Romance

If you are a woman, this card indicates that many people around you will soon want you. If you are a man, this card indicates that you will soon find someone who will leave an impression on you. If you are in a relationship, this card indicates that you will have great sex in the next few days to come.

Profession

This card indicates that you will soon come across an opportunity that will improve your position in your job. You will receive information to help you climb the ladder with ease. This card indicates inspiration and creativity. If you are a student, the card's appearance during your reading indicates you will have a good teacher shortly. You must make sure not to discuss your finances with everybody. Give people only the information they need to know.

Health

This card indicates that you should listen to what your body has to say to you when it comes to health. You must learn to identify the signals your body leaves for you to understand what needs to be done. If this appears in your reading, it means you and the people around you are not concerned about your health. Do not let people ignore your feelings and emotions.

Spirituality

This card indicates wisdom and spirituality. If the card appears during a reading, it is time for you to connect with your intuition and inner voice. This is the only way you can trust the higher power. This card is another great indicator of your psychic abilities.

Reversed Position

Key Meanings

Lack of self-belief, unwanted attention, repression of intuition, uncontrolled sexual tension, sporadic outbursts, fertility issues, blocked psychic powers.

General Interpretation

In the upright and reversed positions, this card indicates that you should trust your intuition, and it will guide you if you listen to it. However, the card in this position indicates that you are not paying attention to your intuition. You are probably focusing more on what people around you think. You want to please them regardless of what your intuition has to say. If this card appears in your reading, it means you are not taking care of yourself. Learn to trust your intuition because you have all the knowledge and wisdom you need.

Romance

If this card appears in the reading, it means that people around you will want you, but you will question their motives. You will not like the attention they shower on you. If you are in a relationship, you may have sexual tension and emotional outbursts. You may soon lose patience and will look for a way to argue with your partner. This card indicates you need to give yourself time.

Profession

This card indicates that you are not being kept in the loop in the current project. It also indicates that the people at work do not care for your inputs. They may isolate you, and this leaves you feeling unwanted. This card also means there are duplicitous people around you, and you should maintain a close circle. Make sure to read every document placed in front of you before you sign a contract or take a loan. If it does not feel right, then do not do it.

Health

This card in the reversed position means you are lazy and need to be active. The card may also indicate menstruation issues in women and other issues, such as fertility issues and hormonal imbalances. Try different methods and treatments if the methods do not help you.

Spirituality

If this card appears in your reading, it means you are no longer in touch with your spirituality. Your intuition knows what you need to do, but you cannot grasp the message. Also, make sure you do not depend entirely on mediums or psychics to decipher these messages.

The Empress

Upright Position

Key Meanings

Fertility, pregnancy, sensuality, creativity, motherhood, femininity, art, harmony, beauty, nature

General Interpretation

This card indicates motherhood and femininity. This is one of the strongest cards in the major arcana, and if it comes in your reading, it means you will soon find fulfillment. If you are a parent, this card indicates that you should learn to communicate well with your kids. Even if you are not a kid, and this card appears in your reading, it means you should embrace the soft side of your personality. Explore your emotions and trust your intuition. People around you will be drawn to you since you are compassionate, empathetic, and calm.

Romance

This card is extremely positive, and if you are single and see it in your reading, it indicates that love will find you. If you are already in a relationship, it means you will be committed to each other and more affectionate and loving. This card also indicates good sex. If you enjoy the romance in your current relationship, remember that this card is a strong pregnancy indicator. If you are not ready to be a parent, take the necessary precautions.

Profession

If this card appears in your reading, it means you will inspire everybody around you. You will feel creative and passionate about your work. Your creativity will help you develop new ideas, and if you are looking for a change in role, this will be the best time to do it. This card indicates that your finances will be healthy, and there is a steady cash inflow, so it is the right time to invest in shares and other investment options. When you reap these investments' benefits, you should learn to share the reward with those who most need it.

Health

This card indicates pregnancy, so if you are trying to get pregnant, this card indicates success. If you do not want to get pregnant but can get pregnant, you need to exercise caution. This card also acts as a warning – if you are not looking to get pregnant and pick up this card during a reading, it means you are not nurturing yourself enough. You must take time out of your schedule to unwind and relax. This is the only way you can manage your energy levels.

Spirituality

When this card appears in your reading, it indicates that you need to focus on your intuition and listen to it. Take time to relax and listen to what your intuition is saying to you. Remember that your intuition is right, and if you have not been doing this until now, start now. When this card appears in your reading, you know you can connect with your subconscious mind or higher power. When you do this, you can connect better with the cards.

Reversed Position

Key Meanings

Lack of confidence, infertility, lack of growth, negligence, overbearing tendencies, insecurity, and disharmony

General Interpretation

If the card appears in the reverse position during a reading, it indicates you should accept your feminine qualities. It is important to remember that everybody has a mixture of feminine and masculine qualities. This card in the reversed position indicates you have neglected your feminine characteristics and qualities. This is especially true for men since they tend to ignore their feminine characteristics. Try to focus more on things that matter in life rather than the mental and material aspects of your life. This causes disharmony that will make it harder for you to think about others for a change. You may also be emotionally overwhelmed. Your confidence may also take a hit, and you may not find yourself attractive. This is when you need to focus on the ground and balance the energies within yourself.

Romance

When this card shows up in your reading, it means there are many people pursuing you, but they do not know the real you since you are afraid to show them who you are. Do not pretend to be someone else only because you want to gain the approval of the person in whom you are interested. If you are in a relationship, this card means you are not true to your partner. You are keeping your emotions at bay so you can balance the relationship. Maybe you fear rejection if you reveal your true feelings to your partner. Take time to think about what you want from the relationship and why you are suppressing your emotions. Always be mindful of your behavior since you can be overbearing. This is only because of your insecurities. The easiest way to overcome these emotions is to shift the focus back on your thoughts and emotions. Let your intuition and inner thoughts guide you to become the inspiring, beautiful, and confident person you are.

Profession

This card in this position indicates that you no longer like your work. It has become a part of your routine and is monotonous because you want to move into a creative field. You are probably not appreciated enough at work, but this need not be the case. Your emotions and thoughts make you feel this way. Do not make hasty decisions regarding your career, especially if you are not up for it yet. Spend time to understand the problem and the root of it. You may have enough money, but you do not feel confident about it. Make the right choices, so you are secure financially in the long run.

Health

The card indicates that you need to focus on your health and take care of yourself. This card in the reversed position means you will have emotional conflicts that will lead to binge eating, laziness, lethargy, and apathy, so do everything you can to make yourself feel better about yourself. If you place this card in this position during your reading, it indicates pregnancy and infertility issues.

Spirituality

When this card appears in your reading in terms of spirituality, it means you no longer connect with your intuition. This means various aspects of your life will also not function the way you need them to. It is important for you to reconnect with your intuition, so you find the link that will help you overcome any issues in your life.

The Emperor

Upright Position

Key Meanings

Stability, father figure, protectiveness, practical, authority, older man, fatherhood, dependability, practical, structure, logical

General Interpretation

If you look at the card carefully, you can see that the Emperor is an older man. The card indicates that the person is good at work and possibly wealthy. If this card appears in your reading, it means you are a grounded and powerful protector, but you can also be stubborn and rigid. Alternatively, the card can indicate to the person you are currently in a relationship with. This card indicates that the individual does not like having fun and would rather spend time on work. The Emperor's children often fall short of his expectations, and they tend to have self-esteem issues.

If you pull the card and place it in the past position, it means you had an authoritarian father figure in your life. He did have your best interests but could rarely shower you with love and affection. If the card does appear in the future or present positions, it means someone is watching out for you – a person will give you the right advice to help you improve your life.

If the card resembles nobody in your life, it can signify that you trust logic over emotion. The card signifies focus, stability, concentration, and structure you need in life to succeed.

Romance

If you are interested in men and single, the appearance of this card in your reading can mean you will find yourself romantically involved with an older man. This individual will like order, routine, logic, and structure. Since he is more stoic than romantic, he cannot show affection. He is protective, practical, and dependable. If you are single and interested in women, this card indicates you need to be more open with your emotions. If you are interested in someone, do not wait for them to approach you. Go break the ice and let them know how you feel. This card indicates monogamy; if you have had trouble in your relationship in the past, this card indicates that it will improve in the days to come.

Profession

If the Emperor card has appeared in your reading, it indicates that people will recognize your hard work and appreciate you. Perseverance, concentration, and focus are the only means to succeed in life. If you are looking for a new job, you must be persistent in your search. You need to use logic when you apply for any position. Trust that the right opportunities will come your way, and you will have structure in your career. The card can also indicate that an older team member or boss will support and guide you. With your finances, this card indicates that you need to be practical and responsible with your finances. Control your spending and always know where the money is going. This does not mean you need to control every penny that goes out of your pocket, but you need to avoid any unnecessary spending.

Health

This card indicates that you are not giving yourself enough rest. Stop performing any unnecessary activities, especially those that cause more harm to your body. You no longer have to exercise for hours but should learn to be kind to your body. If you suffer from an illness, this card's appearance in your reading indicates that you are treating the illness correctly. Do not try to suck it up and move on with life because that will not help you. If your body indicates you need rest, go take a rest. If you are unwell, seek treatment immediately and listen to what the doctor says.

Spirituality

This card signifies that you are not paying attention to your intuition. You are focusing more on the material part of your life. Do not let your logic overshadow your sensitive side. Spend time to focus on your spirituality. If you are working hard on your spirituality, this card's appearance in your reading can indicate you need to work on protecting and grounding yourself.

Reversed Position

Key Meanings

Controlling, obsessive, abuse of power, lack of discipline, father issues, lack of control, stubbornness, absentee father, rigidity

General Interpretation

If the card in the reversed position appears in your reading, it signifies that someone in your life with authority and power is abusing their position. This leaves you feeling rebellious or powerless. Having said that, the person is trying to give you the right advice and guide you, but their words are lost because of their behavior. The easiest way to deal with this is to be patient and calm. Only listen to the advice that works best for you and ignore the rest.

Always stand up to the way the person is behaving with you, but always do it in the right way. Lashing out at them will not get you the results you need. This card also indicates that the person you looked upon as a father figure has abandoned or let you down. If the card represents no individual in your life, it can mean you are letting your thoughts and emotions guide you. You must try to balance your emotions and logic. The card in this position indicates that you need to have structure in life.

Romance

This card in the reversed position indicates there is an imbalance in your relationship. It is this imbalance causing unhappiness and conflict. The card can also indicate that one person in the relationship is possessive, overbearing, stubborn, and controlling. This behavior only leads to a feeling of being trapped. This card in the reversed position shows there is a lack of balance in the relationship, especially because of the controlling nature, so both you and your partner need to find a balance.

If you are single, this card can indicate that your paternity issues are causing a destructive pattern for choosing your partner. Find a way to resolve these issues, so you can attract the right people. Your destructive thought patterns only invite people who want to take advantage of you. The card also indicates that you fear commitment and rebel against every characteristic of the Emperor.

Profession

If the card appears in the reversed position, it shows you lack focus and consistency for working. You find that the rules at work bother you and you need to change your place of work soon. There may be a different job in the same industry or another that offers more freedom. You may not want to follow orders and want to be your boss. Consider these options. With your finances, this card indicates that you lack control and need to get help from a professional.

Health

The card indicates you are not giving yourself enough time to rest and recuperate. You have a hectic routine that only causes stress. This routine can cause poor sleeping patterns, headaches, and other physical symptoms. You should not push your body too far since that will only lead to injury. Rest enough. If you have been taking good care of yourself, the card can indicate that you need to set a routine to improve your health.

Spirituality

In terms of spirituality, the card indicates that you should explore a different path to search for your spirituality. You should explore different paths, but you must ensure you trust and focus on yourself, even if you do come in contact with spiritual advisors.

The Hierophant

Upright Position

Key meanings

Traditional values, knowledge sharing, conformity, commitment, traditional institutions, marriage, conventional beliefs, religion

General Interpretation

This card represents institutions and traditional values. The card can either represent a mentor or counselor willing to provide you with guidance and wisdom. Alternatively, it can represent a religious or spiritual advisor, such as a rabbi, imam, vicar, priest, monk, or preacher who will guide you regarding your spirituality. When this card appears in your reading, it can mean you are constantly in touch with people who are stubborn about their beliefs and thoughts. The various institutions this card can represent include tradition, convention, religion, economy, family, social, social welfare, educational, medical, political, etc. The appearance of the card signifies that you should conform to tradition or convention. You should not try to rock the boat, but you *should* participate in ceremonies or create new traditions for yourself.

Romance

If you are in a relationship, this card's appearance in your reading indicates commitment and marriage. You can expect the relationship to move towards new milestones. The card indicates that the relationship is balanced on the same goals and values. If you are looking to answer a question on commitment, your relationship will turn a new leaf if this card appears in your reading. If you are single, it indicates you will begin a relationship based on security, commitment, and love soon.

Profession

If the card appears in your reading, it means you should start working with a team. Always do what is expected of you and do not focus on any unconventional methods. This is the only way to guarantee success. The card signifies that you will find a mentor or teacher who will share his knowledge with you. This knowledge will help you in your career. You can also become a mentor or trainer for your team. When this card appears in your reading, it can mean it is time for you to study at an established university. This is an excellent time to invest in conventional investment plans to avoid any risk. Try to stick to the conventional method of managing your money. Speak to an expert if you need advice on how to manage your finances.

Health

If you have any health issues, this card indicates that you should try to use conventional medicine. This is the best route for you. It is also a good time to set up a health routine in your life, such as taking vitamin supplements or exercising regularly. This is one of the easiest ways to boost your immune system.

Spirituality

Since the card represents spirituality, the archetype is considered the link between the higher power and you. If this card appears in your reading, it indicates there will be a spiritual advisor entering your life to help you on your journey. While this card is often associated with traditional beliefs and practices, if you do not believe or follow any traditional religion, the appearance of the card in your reading means you need to build a ritual into your spiritual practice.

Reversed Position
Key Meaning

Unconventional lifestyle, non-conformity, challenging beliefs and traditions, reversed roles, unconventional relationships

General Interpretation

When this card appears in the reversed position in your reading, it means you should break convention soon. You may want to change the rigid rules, traditional structure, and social norms, so it benefits everybody. The people around you will not understand why you are challenging things, and they may be against it, but this will not stop you from doing what you think is right. You will think for yourself and get rid of any traditional practices and beliefs that do not help you.

The card in the reversed position indicates you want to choose an alternative lifestyle of the way of living. The card's appearance in your reading can also mean you are clinging to all the traditional ways because you are ashamed or guilty. This will only lead to your detriment. Only when you learn to live the way you want can you free yourself from oppression. This experience will help you develop positively. The card in the reversed position can also mean you will clash with people in authority.

Romance

When this card appears in your reading in the reversed position, it means you want to be in an unconventional relationship or are already in one. You probably do not want to get married and are breaking tradition. You may also be in a relationship where the roles are reversed, and the people around you may constantly wonder or question your relationship. Alternatively, the card can also indicate that you and your partner are not seeing eye-to-eye, which is causing insecurity and conflict between the two of you. You need to be open and understand what your partner has to say. It is important to understand that compromise does not mean you need to push yourself out of your comfort zone.

Profession

If this card appears in your reading, it means you work with people who are rigid with rules. They never budge and always want people to do things their way. If this individual is your boss, you will no longer like to work in the same organization since you will constantly be at war with this individual. If you work with a group of people, it can mean that the team may ask you to listen to what the majority has to say despite their decisions' going against your beliefs. You may also find a mentor or teacher who may teach you how to challenge things in life.

Health

If you have been ill for some time, the appearance of this card in your reading is a sign you should try holistic or alternative therapies. These courses will benefit you and heal you faster than traditional medication, so do not be too rigid and change things a little. Find those therapies that work best for you. You may need to think out of the box.

Spirituality

When this card appears in your reading in the reversed position, it means you should let go of those traditional beliefs, especially the ones you no longer benefit from. Also, find the path that best suits you. You never have to follow traditional beliefs to be spiritual.

The Lovers

Upright Position

Key Meanings

Soulmates, love, partnerships, major choices, sexual connections, relationships, kindred spirits, shared values, desire, perfect unions

General Interpretation

This card signifies harmony, attraction, a perfect union, and love. If this card appears in your reading, it signifies that you are finding the balance in yourself. You have finally understood what you want and need. You also have a clear idea about your morals and beliefs and know what you value. This is one of the best ways to bring peace and balance to life.

When this card appears in your reading, it indicates that you will make a major decision. You are probably uncertain about people and situations in life, but the appearance of this card indicates that you will succeed in life. You will soon know what direction you need to take in life. Since these are important decisions, avoid taking the easy road. You must ensure you have the required information and choose the right path. This may seem difficult, but it is the only way to achieve great things in life.

Romance

If you are looking for love or relationship advice, this is the best card in the deck. This card is a soulmate card, and it talks about the bond that people share. If you are in a relationship, this card is a sign you and your partner will rekindle the relationship. The bond between the two of you will deepen, and you will learn to be more open to everything in your relationship. If you are single, this card indicates that you will find love soon. This relationship will not be infatuation alone, but you will love and respect each other. There will also be a deep and mutual understanding between the two of you. This card represents everything good about a relationship.

Profession

When this card appears in the upright position, it means you and your partner can start your company. If you have always wanted to start a company, this is the right time. You and your business partner are on the same page and can work together to set up the company. The two of you can support each other fully.

If this card arises in your reading, it indicates that you may find yourself romantically involved with a teammate or colleague. However, you should understand the risks and issues involved with mixing pleasure and business. This card also signifies that you need to decide about your career path. The decisions you need to make may seem undesirable, but this may not be the case. Gather all your facts and make the right decisions – a change in your role, a job change, etc. You should welcome these changes.

Health

If you have health issues, then this card indicates that you have the right support to overcome those issues. This support can either be a friend or partner supporting you. It can also indicate a healthcare provider or doctor treating you. This card can indicate that you have made the right decisions that will improve your health quickly. The card also relates to your heart health, so you must ensure you take good care of your health and heart when you find this card in your reading.

Spirituality

When this card appears in the upright position, it means you are working on finding a balance between your thoughts, actions, and emotions. This can only happen when you understand yourself better. This shows you your personal morals and beliefs, which leads to a stronger connection between your physical and spiritual self. This card in the upright position indicates you need to find a partner, so you can begin your spiritual journey together. You can take a meditation or yoga class together.

Reversed Position

Key Meanings

Trust issues, conflict, disharmony, lack of accountability, detachment, disconnection, imbalance, disunion

General Interpretation

This card indicates that you may be struggling to own up to your decisions. This only leads to conflict and uncertainty. You will never know where your life is headed. Remember that you can control your destiny. Never blame the higher power or energy, especially if you are the cause of your problems. Learn to be accountable for your mistakes and learn from your past mistakes. Learn to let things go. You also need to find a way to move ahead in the right way. Understand yourself better. Identify your beliefs and values, so you do not repeat the same mistakes.

Romance

If this card appears in the reversed position and you are in a relationship, it means the intimacy is great between you and your partner, but it means that the two of you are not on the same page when it comes to other important areas of your relationship. You both do not trust each other completely, and this makes it hard for the two of you to jump into the relationship fully. You probably have different values, hopes, and goals for the future, which makes it difficult for the two of you to connect. If you are unsure of the reason, consider the supporting cards to confirm the cause of the problem. Regardless of the reason, you both need to work on sorting the difference to ensure the survival of the relationship. If you are single, it means you will find the person you want to be in a relationship with, but this may not happen as soon as you had hoped. This card also means you probably choose the wrong people as your partners because you are unsure why you want to be with someone. This card indicates that you need to find a way to connect with a person before you jump into a relationship.

Profession

This card indicates there is disharmony between you and your partners. If you cannot communicate with your business partner, sit down with them and decide what you want to do with the business. Find the path your business will take. Find a balance with your partner so your business does not take a hit. This card indicates that you may find love at work, but you need to be cautious about it since this can only lead to trouble. It is important for you to understand the consequences of mixing your professional and personal life. When this card appears, it indicates that you will make impulsive decisions, and this can only lead to instant gratification, but learn to be accountable and avoid making the same mistakes repeatedly.

Health

With health, this card indicates you should learn to connect with your body and strike a balance between your health and harmony. You may feel that your body is not working for you but against you, but you need to learn to be kind to yourself. You also need to work with the current energy levels. Your body can do a lot for you, but sometimes, it needs rest. Never let your frustration get the better of you. Just give it time to heal.

Spirituality

With the spiritual aspect, this card in the reversed position indicates that you are only focusing on materialistic aspects of life. You want to fulfill all your dreams. This behavior will help you feel better, but this is only a temporary situation. It never helps you find peace and harmony. Always focus on the spiritual side and learn more about the true you. This is a better way to reward yourself. When this card is reversed, it indicates that you are sexually attracted to one of your spiritual advisors. If this advisor is seeking a relationship with you, then it means they are only doing this to abuse their power. This individual should guide your every move and help you on your journey. So, if they approach you differently, then you should be cautious.

The Chariot

Upright Position

Key Meanings

Hard work, focus, ambition, success, willpower, victory, determination, overcoming obstacles, self-discipline and control

General Interpretation

This card indicates that you can overcome various obstacles in life through focus, willpower, and determination. When this card appears in your reading, it indicates that you will feel in control, ambitious, and motivated. It is finally time for you to do everything you wanted to, but this card does not come without its challenges. You may face obstacles on the way, but you can overcome them if you stay focused. The card can also indicate that you may travel soon. It may feel like you are constantly at the battle, but do not worry since success is right around the corner.

Romance

When this card appears during a love reading, it indicates that you should work on conquering your emotions. This must be done if you want the relationship to succeed. If you have been going through a rough patch in your relationship, this card's appearance indicates you need to work with your partner to overcome your issues. If you are single, this card indicates that you need to let go of your past relationships, especially to move ahead in life.

Profession

When this card appears in your reading, it indicates that you are motivated and ambitious. If you have trouble with your colleagues, this card indicates that you need to stop worrying about people trying to sabotage you and focus on your work. If you are looking for a job, you may soon get the job you want. In terms of finances, this card is a good omen since it represents overcoming obstacles. Now is a good time to target any investments and purchases.

Health

If you have had health issues in the past, you will find the motivation to tackle those issues. You may take time to recover fully, but your willpower and energy will help to overcome these challenges.

Spirituality

In terms of spirituality, this card represents the start of a spiritual journey. You will have your fair share of obstacles and hurdles, but you can achieve success. Stay focused and be strong enough to try new things.

Reversed Position

Key Meanings

Being blocked by obstacles, lack of self-control, coercion, aggression, powerlessness, and forcefulness

General Interpretation

When the card appears in the reversed position, it indicates that you lack direction and feel powerless, so you need to control your destiny and never let outside forces change your course of action. Learn to control your life and do not go with the flow. You may lack confidence and feel powerless, which could lead to frustration and anger. Be determined to understand what course of action you need to take and the boundaries you want to set.

Romance

According to this card, you need to slow down. If you are in a relationship not progressing the way you would like it to, you must be patient. Trust that your relationships will progress the way they need to. Do not force things. If you feel like your relationship will move to the next stage, let it run its course. Do not be coerced into doing things you do not want. If you are single, the card indicates you will meet someone soon. While you should cherish the joy the relationship brings, do not rush into it.

Profession

You will still be motivated, but it indicates that you are not pacing your path when the card is in the reversed position. Take one step at a time. Let things run their course, and stop forcing your approach since this will be detrimental only to you.

Health

This card in the reversed position signifies that you will have a burst of energy and motivation. Do not rush into anything but take things slowly. If you are starting an exercise program, remember to take it slow. Do not do too much because you may end up hurting yourself.

Spirituality

The chariot indicates that you are ready to take on your spiritual journey. You must be mindful to never focus too hard on meeting all your goals. Let your spiritual path guide you and accept the rewards written in your name.

The Strength

Upright Position

Key Meanings

Overcoming self-doubt, control, taming, confidence, bravery, courage, inner strength, and compassion

General Interpretation

This card is associated with inner strength. When this card appears in your reading, it indicates that you can overcome any situation in life by mastering your emotions and thoughts. This card represents the strength you have to overcome challenges, similar to the Chariot, but his card only represents inner strength. This card indicates that you are strong enough to overcome any troubles and fears you may have. Since you are skilled, you can achieve success easily.

Romance

This card represents the constellation Leo. This means you can expect to have a relationship with a Leo if this card does come up in your reading. If you are single, this card indicates that you will meet someone soon. This is exciting news, but you need to see if the person is too wild for you. If you are in a relationship, this card indicates that you are a strong couple.

Profession

In terms of career, this card indicates that you should now work on mastering your fears, emotions, and thoughts, so you can forge ahead. You have the potential and all the skills you need to achieve this. Never let the fear of failure hold you back. To be promoted, then do everything you can so nobody overlooks you. With finances, you must make sure that you do not spend too much. The objective is to avoid making impulsive decisions.

Health

When you need a question on your health answered, this is a great card to get. This card indicates that your health is improving or that you are fit. If you have been ill, this card indicates that you will get your strength back soon. This card's appearance in your reading indicates that it is time for you to improve your lifestyle.

Spirituality

In terms of spirituality, this card indicates that you will connect with your spiritual self soon. This connection will help you find your inner balance and drive you forward to help you achieve your dreams. If you have had a few difficult days, this card indicates that you have the strength to overcome any obstacle.

Reversed Position

Key meanings

Feeling inadequate, low self-esteem, self-doubt, lack of confidence, vulnerability, and weakness.

General Interpretation

When this card appears in the reversed position, it indicates that you are not using the right strength to overcome obstacles. This card does not indicate that you are letting your fear control you. It is time for you to trust your inner strength to help you get out of a rut. You must find the strength to get out of your current situation. Always focus on the positive.

Romance

This card in the reversed position indicates that you are unresolved. You have self-esteem issues and cannot control your thoughts and impulses. This will always make you choose the wrong things in life. This becomes a vicious circle since a bad relationship will only scar you. Never let your fear or anxiety cause any problems in a relationship where there are no issues.

Profession

This card in the reversed position almost means the same thing as the card in the upright position. The card indicates you need to trust yourself and move ahead in your career. In the reversed position, this card indicates that you have always let your fear control you. Trust you have the strength to overcome any issues. Focus on your goals and work towards your end goal. When you are confident, people will be drawn to you, and they will notice the change. You may have an abundance of wealth at the moment, but this will not last if you are not smart.

Health

In terms of health, this card indicates that you are in good health, but you may lack self-control that can harm your body. Overcome these bad habits. Make small changes.

Spirituality

When this card appears in the reversed position, it indicates that you are connected to your spirit. Your emotions and fears stop you from connecting with your spirit. You need to find a way to let go of these fears.

The Hermit

Upright Position

Key Meanings

Solitude, soul searching, introspection, inner guidance, self-reflection, and contemplation

General Interpretation

This card in the upright position indicates that you have entered the period where you will attain spiritual enlightenment. You will find time to understand yourself better and remove yourself from your routine to understand your spiritual self. This card can also indicate that you want to isolate or withdraw to recover from hardships. This card indicates that you need to focus on yourself and your needs before focusing on helping others.

Romance

If you are single, this card indicates that you will find someone soon. You are coming out of the period of solitude and loneliness. You have had enough time to recuperate from a previous heartbreak. If you are in a relationship, this card indicates that you need to try to spend time with your partner.

Profession

This card indicates that you are focusing on making money and your career. You are looking only at materialistic pursuits and ignore activities that leave you happy. This card also indicates that you may wonder if you have chosen the right career. With your finances, it is time for you to be mature and invest carefully.

Health

This card indicates that you are overdoing things that can lead to injury. Take time out to breathe. Relax and rejuvenate your health. Take a minute every day to calm yourself and connect with your body. This is the best way to improve your health.

Spirituality

This card indicates that you should work on your spirituality now. You can choose any activity to help you connect with your spirit. Isolate yourself to do this. Focus on your spiritual side and give yourself time to listen to your inner spirit.

Reversed Position

Key Meanings

Paralyzed by fear, isolation, withdrawal, loneliness, being reclusive, restrictive, paranoia, and anti-social

General Interpretation

This card, in the reverse position, indicates that you have become reclusive. You may have had to remain alone for a short period, but you need to come back to the world and meet the people in your life. You can take time for soul-searching if you need to, but you also need to do it in moderation. You need to learn to draw the line at some point and determine if what you are doing is what you need to do.

Romance

This card in the reverse position indicates that you are lonely. If you are single, it suggests that you do not want to be in a relationship since you feel like you have missed your window. If you are in a relationship, it indicates that you feel like your partner is shutting you out. This card, in the reverse position, can indicate that you and your partner need to talk and communicate with each other.

Profession

In terms of career, this card indicates that you need to put yourself out there, network, and work on restoring business connections. You cannot work in solitude forever. It is best to work with teams and interact with the right people. This card suggests that you should make the right investment choices now with your finances.

Health

This card in the reversed position indicates that you may have mental health issues. The card is also a warning you need to give yourself time to relax.

Spirituality

When this card appears in the reverse position, it indicates that you spend time alone. You need to develop an interest in various activities so you develop spiritually. It is great to work alone when it comes to spiritual work, but it is also a good idea to connect with others.

The Wheel of Fortune

Upright Position

Key Meanings

Chance, destiny, cycles of life, upheaval, and fate

General Interpretation

This card indicates there are big changes coming your way. These changes are good for you, but change can never be easy. This is true even in the case that the change leads you to your destiny. The card in the upright position indicates that the universe is helping you achieve your goals. The card also indicates that your life is constantly changing.

Romance

If you are single, this card indicates that the universe is using its power to bring you closer to the person you are meant to be with. This suggests that you will have great fortune when it comes to love. If you are in a relationship, this card indicates that you and your partner may be ready to take the next step. This card can also mean there are difficulties that will creep into your life.

Profession

In terms of your career, this card is a good omen. It means you can expect changes in your job. If you have wanted to change your career or start your business, now is a good time. The universe will do everything it can to help you meet your goals. If you are stable and happy, this card indicates there will be big changes coming your way. These changes can be challenging, but they will lead to bigger things. With your finances, this card indicates that you will be comfortable. If you have had money problems, this card's appearance in your reading will indicate that things will improve for you.

Health

With your health, this card indicates that your health will improve if you have had health issues. You may also need to change your lifestyle. If you have been pushing yourself too far physically, emotionally, and mentally, it is time to slow down now.

Spirituality

This card indicates that fate is on your side. Spend time every day working on your spirituality. Use different exercises to help you develop and grow. Trust the universe and accept the signs it sends your way. This is the only way you can ensure that your situation improves.

Reversed Position

Key Meanings

Setbacks, external forces, unwelcome change, disorder, back luck, disruption, and upheaval

General Interpretation

This card, in the reverse position, indicates there will be a change in your life. This change is possibly unwelcome and negative. This card indicates that you will have challenging times, and it is time for you to adjust to this change. This change may make it seem like you have no control over your life. But this is not the case. When this happens, you need to take control of your life and situation. Learn from your past. Things may seem tough now, but there is a bright future ahead of you.

Romance

If you are single, take this time to understand yourself better. You may need to learn from your past mistakes and ensure you find happiness. You choose what you want to learn from your life. If you are in a relationship, this card indicates that your relationship is stagnant. You will find that the sparkle has gone out of the relationship, and you need to work on improving your relationship.

Profession

With your career, this card indicates that your career has stagnated. It also suggests there is uncertainty in your career. This card, in the reverse position, shows there are unwelcome changes coming your way, so you need to assess all the decisions you want to make about your career and see if you are making the right decisions. Understand this situation is temporary. Learn from the past and carry the lessons with you. This card indicates that you have not been careful with your money and need to set up a safety net for yourself in terms of finances.

Health

In terms of health, this card in the reversed position indicates you find disruption and issues in other areas of your life, creating a problem elsewhere. Never let pessimism get in the way. Change is often stressful, but realize that change is constant. You can determine how you will let the situation affect you.

Spirituality

With your spirituality, this card indicates that you may feel overwhelmed. You may feel the universe is not working in your favor. This will test your faith but remember that the universe has a plan for you. The trouble will pass, and you will come out more connected to your spirit.

The Justice

Upright Position

Key Meanings

Life lessons, karmic justice, legal disputes, honesty, truth, justice, and integrity

General Interpretation

As the card's name suggests, this card is related to legal matters, cause and effect, and justice. This card shows you that every action you perform has its own consequences, so you need to look at the situation and see what actions you have performed to bring you there. This card is also related to balance. This card signifies that your circumstances may change soon. Things may be out of your control, but it is your doing. Do not let the situation overwhelm you.

Romance

If you are single, this card indicates that you may find yourself in a relationship with a person working in the legal industry. This card corresponds to the Libra constellation. This means you may find a Libra in your life soon. If you have had trouble in your past relationships, this card indicates that your troubles will soon be over. You will emerge happier in the current relationship. If you are already in a relationship, the effect of this card's energy depends on how you and your partner behave.

Profession

If this card appears in a career reading, it suggests that you should pay attention to your life. You need to balance your personal life and work. Always take time out for yourself. True work and money are important, but not at the cost of letting go of some of your dreams. Make time for the people important to you.

Health

If you have had health issues in the past, this card indicates that you may be out of balance. It also suggests that you need to stop overindulging in some areas of your life.

Spirituality

In terms of your spirituality, this card indicates that you should focus on karma. This does not mean you will be punished for past mistakes. It only means you need to learn certain lessons in life, and the universe is helping you learn them.

Reversed Position

Key Meanings

Karmic avoidance, karmic retribution, injustice, unfairness, dishonesty

General Interpretation

When this card appears in the reverse position, it indicates injustice. This injustice can take different forms. It could mean you are being treated unfairly at work, and this affects you. It could also mean that people are treating you differently for no fault of your own. There may be a case where you were caught in a lie. So, do not let this happen. Ensure that you are honest if you are ever caught in a lie. Dishonesty only makes the situation worse.

Love and Relationship

If you are single, this card indicates that you are ready for a relationship, especially one you deserve. However, you have not learned from your past relationships, which makes it difficult for you to move on. You also make the same mistakes in your relationship because you have not learned. You may get caught up in the beauty of new love, but this does not help you. Take the relationship slowly.

If you are in a relationship, this position indicates that you are cheating or lying to your partner and will soon be caught. You can expect grave consequences. Any argument between you and your partner also may seem endless.

Profession

In terms of your career, this card indicates that you are not being treated fairly by the people around you. People may blame you for their mistakes, and there are times you may want to react but don't. You need to hold back and find the right way to deal with these people. This card, in the reverse position, also indicates that you have not been acting with integrity. Your behavior will cause problems. Do not avoid these consequences but learn from your mistakes. This is the only way you earn your respect.

Health

This card indicates that you need to find a balance between your personal and professional lives in terms of health. Spend some time everyday rejuvenating.

Spirituality

This card, in the reverse position, indicates that the universe is sending you learnings. You may be avoiding these learnings since you fear what may happen to you. You cannot refuse to learn these lessons since the universe will ensure you learn them in a bigger way.

Chapter Six: Cards 12 – 21

The Hanged Man

Upright Position

Key Meanings

Letting go, self-limiting, lack of direction, feeling trapped, needing release, confined.

General Interpretation

This card, in the upright position, indicates that you are in an unhappy situation. You feel like you are stuck in a rut or trapped. However, you fail to realize that you have the power to bring yourself out of this situation. You need only to change the way you look at the situation, and this will help you overcome all obstacles. This card also signifies that you are unsure of what direction you should take. It is important to remember that you cannot control every aspect of your life, and you need to let things take their course.

Romance

When this card appears in your reading, it suggests that you are not happy in your current relationship. It indicates that you need to step back and reevaluate your relationship. This helps you determine where your relationship is heading. This card suggests that you should make no decisions about your relationship now but need to think about the situation. If you are truly unhappy, you can let the relationship go. If you are single, the card suggests that you should let people; situations, or ideas go if they make you unhappy.

Profession

This card indicates that you should not feel uncertain about your job or career. If it has become stagnant, identify the steps you need to take to move ahead in your profession. Relax and let things take their course. If you rush, you will make the wrong decision. Your anxiety makes you feel like you have nothing when you actually do have enough to survive regarding finances.

Health

If you have been experiencing some health issues, this card suggests that you should consider every treatment option available to you. Do not reject the treatment you are undertaking but rethink the way you are tackling the problem. This card also indicates that the issue you are experiencing will take time to heal. So, do not get frustrated.

Spirituality

With the spiritual context, this card tells you that you should be careful about how you think of yourself. Stop engaging in negative thoughts and emotions since they affect the way you feel about life. You need to think positively and let go of thoughts and beliefs that do not work for you. This is the only way a whole new world opens up for you.

Reversed Position

Key Meanings

Stagnation, apathy, negative patterns, detachment

General Interpretation

This card, in the reverse position, indicates that you are only making wrong decisions. You are doing this because you want to distract yourself or change the way your life is. This card indicates that you are jumping from one situation and another without looking at how your actions are affecting you. Your attitude towards yourself and life will determine how you lead your life.

Romance

If you are in a relationship, this card indicates that you and your partner are holding back from each other. The two of you are only stuck to each other because you do not want to start over. The card also indicates that you can salvage the relationship, but you cannot confront these issues. If you are single, it indicates that you are sticking to the negative patterns only. You have not learned from your mistakes. Determine the pattern and try to work around it.

Profession

This card indicates that your career is not going in the direction you want it to when it comes to work. The card also suggests that you do not want to deal with the uncertainties. You may resort to blame the people around you and feel like you cannot change the current situation for yourself. This is the best time to control your life. Determine what you want to do and choose to do it. You may also need to gain a fresh perspective if needed.

Health

If you are suffering from ill health, this card, in the reverse position, indicates that you should find a way to resolve these issues. You can consider various possibilities and issues in life that are deteriorating your health. For instance, your grief and stress can manifest themselves in different ways in your body. It is best to use holistic or alternative therapies to improve your health.

Spirituality

With your spirituality, the card in the reversed position indicates you no longer know where you are headed. You have become shallow and do not connect to your higher self. This is a good time for you to explore paths to help you manage your situation. This is a good time to engage on a path that will bring you out of a slump. You will connect with your consciousness faster.

The Death

Upright Position

Key Meanings

New beginning, endings, transition, an unexpected upheaval

General Interpretation

This is a card that most people fear because of its name. It, however, does not indicate physical death. When you read tarot, refrain from predicting deaths. This is an irresponsible and unethical act. This card signifies transformation or change. The change may be difficult to undergo, and you may not accept it with an open mind initially. In the end, you will be happy about the change.

Romance

If you are single, this card indicates that you will get rid of your old issues, behavior, and beliefs since they are not useful for you. It is only when you embrace this change you can move ahead in your love life. If you are in a relationship, this card indicates that you are in a relationship you need to let go of. The relationship is no longer working for the two of you, and you are only clinging to old patterns. When this card appears in your reading, it indicates that it is time for you to let go of your relationship.

Profession

With your career, this card can be interpreted as a warning you should not depend on things that are not working for you. Change is always constant. If you are not happy with your job, then it is time for you to look for a new role. Start your business if you want to. When it comes to your finances, you need to be careful about your spending.

Health

As mentioned earlier, do not panic if you see this card in your reading. This card only signifies there will be a change in your health. You know how to handle this change because of your previous experiences. If you had ill health, you might be feeling pessimistic. You should, however, look for something positive and be ready when things change.

Spirituality

The death card represents transformation regarding your spirituality. In a spiritual reading, this card indicates that you can now connect with your spirit. You must learn to embrace this change.

Reversed Position

Key Meanings

Dependency, fear of beginnings, resisting change

General Interpretation

The Death card, in the reverse position, indicates that you are not accepting the change that will help you move forward. You do nothing new in life if you stick to your old beliefs. When you learn to let go, new energy enters your life, and this will lead to a bright beginning. Ask yourself why you are resisting change. If you are afraid, find a way to let go of your fears.

Romance

If you are single, this card indicates that you need to let go of negativity in your life. This is the only way you can bring positivity to your life. Work on your self-esteem and self-confidence. This is the only way you will be happy in life. If you are in a relationship, this card indicates that you want no change in your relationship. You are only clinging to the relationship because you fear being alone. The card also suggests that you can work with your partner to rekindle the flame.

Profession

This card indicates that it is time for you to change your career. You may fear this change because you cannot let go of financial security. Think about what is good for you and work on meeting your goals and dreams. With your finances, work on controlling your spending.

Health

In terms of health, this card indicates that you do not want to improve your health. You do not want to be proactive about your treatments. You may have old fears creeping in but learn to trust your spirit.

Spirituality

This card in the reversed position also signifies transformation. You may be going through a difficult time in life. You, however, do not like change. Have some faith in your spiritual energy and trust you will heal.

The Temperance

Upright Position

Key Meanings

Tranquil, soulmates, inner calm

General Interpretation

This card suggests peace, balance, moderation, and patience. This card indicates you need to find your inner calm and identify the right perspective of things. You need to change the way you look at things and allow yourself to be free of other people's issues. You must identify what you need to do in life and determine your actions.

Romance

If you are single, this indicates you should learn to find a balance in your life. This is the only way the right people will enter your life. If you are in a relationship, you are in a beautiful relationship. If you have had problems in life, this card indicates that you both will resolve the issue.

Profession

In terms of your career, this card indicates that it is a great time for you to set the goals to achieve your dreams. Your dedication and hard work will help you meet your goals. In terms of finance, this card indicates that you have managed your finances well. Having said that, you need to be careful about how you balance your savings.

Health

In terms of health, this card indicates that you need to control any unhealthy habits so you maintain good health. This is a good time for you to do this. If you experience health issues, you must look at the areas where you are not working up to your potential.

Spirituality

In terms of your spirituality, this card tells you that you need to follow your inner guidance. This card suggests that you need to find the right balance between your spirit, mind, and body.

Reversed Position

Key Meanings

Hastiness, clashing, excess, recklessness

General Interpretation

This card in the reversed position indicates an overindulgence or imbalance. This card suggests that you have been behaving in a reckless manner. The card in the reversed position indicates you have lost touch with your inner self and are behaving recklessly. But you are not looking at the bigger picture. You need to step back and see how you behave.

Romance

If you are in a relationship, this card indicates that you may have clashes and conflicts with your partner. This could be because you shower your partner with love, but he does not. There is no harmony in the relationship. So, step back and think about what you need to do. Calm down and reflect on the situation. If you are single, this card indicates that you are very open to people you want to be in a relationship with. Be not hasty and only get together with someone once you know them properly.

Profession

In terms of career, this card indicates there is a conflict at work. You may be working too hard, but the people around you do not appreciate your efforts. Since this frustrates you, you lash out at your co-workers. You need to restore the balance so the situation does not escalate. Regarding your finances, ensure that you do not spend impulsively. Be aware that instant gratification does not keep you happy.

Health

This card indicates that your body is imbalanced, which is leading to various health issues. The card in the reversed position suggests that you are not mindful of what you put into your body. Therefore, you need to connect with your body to determine how you feel and identify the issues causing you discomfort.

Spirituality

In terms of spirituality, this card, in the reverse position, indicates that you have a spiritual imbalance. The card suggests there is an imbalance between soul, body, and mind.

The Devil

Upright Position

Key Meanings

Depression, assault, depression, secrecy

General Interpretation

This card signifies addiction or depression. It may also indicate that you feel restricted or trapped in your relationship. When this card appears in your reading, it indicates that you may feel like external forces restrict you. This will leave you feeling victimized and powerless. Remember that you control your own fate. Therefore, you should never give up. Do not give in to instant gratification since this will not help you.

Romance

If you are single, this card indicates that you will only have an unfulfilling relationship if you are to ever get into one. The relationship may be only sexual, and this does not benefit you or your health. If you are in a relationship, this card indicates that you are trapped in the relationship. You and your partner may be codependent, and this type of relationship is unhealthy for you. If so, you and your partner should step back and determine what needs to be done to change the relationship.

Profession

This card indicates that you are trapped working on projects you do not like in terms of the career. You control your life even if it does not feel this way to you now. Evaluate what you want to do with your career and make the right move. Regarding the money, this card indicates that you should do everything in your power to help you maintain a cushion for the future.

Health

In terms of health, this card indicates that you may have trouble because of your addictions. If you feel you suffer from mental health issues, meet with a professional to discuss the reasons. The card indicates that you need to treat these and not let them define you.

Spirituality

In terms of spirituality, this card indicates you have become materialistic. Work on bringing the focus on yourself and non-materialistic aspects of your life. Do not spend too much time with people who mean nothing to you. It is always important to let go of things. Do not be critical or negative about things in life. Try to find a way to heal any negative feelings you may have.

Reversed Position

Key Meanings

Overcoming addiction, revelation, reasserting control, detachment

General Interpretation

This card in the reversed position indicates that you know *how* you have been trapping yourself in the incorrect things in life. This card indicates that you need to control your life and change the way you think and feel about different situations. The card suggests that you are learning to derive a new perspective from looking at different areas of your life.

Romance

If you are single, this card indicates that you may desperately seek romance. You wanted to be with someone, so you chose to be with whoever was available, no matter how toxic they were for you. The card suggests that you will soon learn to overcome these emotions and learn to be with the right person. If you are in a relationship, you and your partner may feel like you are stuck. It can also indicate that you and your partner did not do something that would end the relationship.

Profession

This card indicates that you know *how* your behavior affects your circumstances in terms of your career. It also indicates that you are finally ready to do what needs to be done to prevent this from happening. You will learn to take the right steps and do what you can to be happy.

Health

The card is a good omen regarding your health since it indicates that you have let go of harmful habits and have started to care more about yourself.

Spirituality

This card indicates that your mindfulness has made it easy for you to prevent any dangerous situations. The card suggests that the universe has let you go since it wants you to learn important lessons without having to go through difficult situations. The card indicates that you are finally coming out of depression, sadness, and anxiety.

The Tower

Upright Position

Key Meanings

Destruction, divorce, disaster

General Interpretation

You should not be wary of the death card but of the tower card since this is the bearer of all bad news. This card indicates that your life will go through a change, and you may not know how to deal with this change. The card suggests that you accept the challenge and face it head-on. This is the only way you can ensure that you have some peace and harmony in life.

Romance

If you are single, you may face a revelation about why you are single. This may not be a nice experience, but it will help you change for the better. If you are in a relationship, this card indicates that you are going through a rough patch. If so, you need to ensure that you let go. If you hold onto a relationship that needs to end, you are only giving yourself more grief.

Profession

This card indicates that you may not be in a secure job. It also signifies loss or redundancy. If this card appears in your reading, it indicates that you may see a change in your profession that will lead to better security and pay.

Health

This card indicates that you may befall an accident, so be careful about your surroundings. This card also suggests that you may have trouble with mental health, and this is understandable since the card indicates that you may go through emotional turmoil. The Tower is only a warning but remember that everything that is to come will pass.

Spirituality

This card represents the removal of old morals and beliefs that do not help you. You may have to reevaluate your beliefs because of an experience you went through. Understand this change will only open you to a new spiritual path.

Reversed Position

Key Meanings

Avoiding loss, delaying the inevitable

General Interpretation

This card in the reversed position indicates that you have avoided a difficult situation. To avoid such situations in life, you need to learn from your experiences. Everybody goes through hardships and learn from them. Do not hold onto those experiences and become bitter. Learn to let go of them and be happy that you came out of it.

Romance

If you are in a relationship, this card indicates that your relationship is over. You are only scared to let go of your partner because of how painful it would be. Face facts and accept things for what they are. If you continue to hold onto a broken relationship, you will only make it difficult for you to be happy. If you are single, this card indicates that you have prevented a disastrous relationship. It also indicates that you do not want to deal with the trauma of previous relationships, and you run away from the idea of a relationship. If so, you need to move on and learn from past relationships.

Profession

In terms of your career, this card indicates that you are working hard despite the difficult circumstances you are in. You may be doing this only to avoid unemployment. If you believe this job is not the right one for you, you should not stick to it because that will only make you unhappy. It is best to be out of your comfort zone so you can do the things you always wanted to.

Health

This card indicates that you have ignored a serious illness under the pretext it will go away. You have to face the illness head-on and see what you can do best to recover.

Spirituality

This card indicates that your old beliefs and morals are false, but you are afraid to let them go. You feel you would not be the person who you are today if you do not have these beliefs. However, you need to accept some facts and let go of those beliefs and morals that no longer help you.

The Sun, Star, and Moon

These cards are the simplest cards to read in the Major Arcana.

The Star

This card is the seventeenth card in the tarot deck, and it indicates swiftness, action, and movement. Some people also term this card as the wish card since it always gives the reader hopeful news. It talks about how a situation can improve and when you will achieve your dreams. The imagery is very easy to interpret. This image radiates a sense of serenity and peace.

If you have trouble with health or find yourself in a stressful relationship, the star's appearance in your reading will indicate a positive change. You need to improve the situation and continue to do better. This card suggests that you need to balance every area of your life. For instance, learn to pay attention to your loved ones and care for your health. This card indicates that you have infinite possibilities in your life. It is an optimistic card that helps you renew trust and faith.

The star also denotes educational and artistic matters, but it also suggests that your creativity will help you in your future endeavors. You will see your health improving if you were suffering from an illness. The star gives you a clear insight into your spirituality. You will finally learn to dive deeper into your inner spirit to learn more about your beliefs and morals.

The Moon

This is the eighteenth card in the major arcana and is associated with ripeness, fullness, and readiness. This card is associated with the constellation Pisces. Each section of the imagery has a significance of its own:

> 1. **Clouds:** Signify your fears and uncertainties
>
> 2. **Water:** Indicates your nature and feelings
>
> 3. **Reflection of the Moon:** Indicates you need to set your fears aside and learn to follow your intuition

When this card appears in your reading, it indicates that you need to listen to the messages from your dreams. This is the only way you can determine what the next course of action should be. The card also indicates that you should not trust people blindly. Be open with people, but not if they can cause harm to you.

The changing light in the imagery indicates that you should always look at the true form. If you are confused about a situation, take some time to understand what you can do to overcome that situation.

The Sun

This is the nineteenth card and is associated with pinnacles and accomplishments. This card's imagery defines everything the card indicates - happiness, enjoyment, love, romance, good health, and more. This card also includes all the elements. When the card appears in your reading, it indicates that you are out of the rut. This card indicates that everything will improve in the days to come.

The Judgment

Upright Position

Key Meanings

Forgiveness, judgment, decisiveness

General Interpretation

This card indicates that people around you are judging you harshly. It also means you are judging people based on how they present themselves. You do not give them time to warm up to you. The card also suggests that you have reached a state of mental clarity that allows you to evaluate yourself.

Romance

If you are in a relationship, this card indicates that you and your partner are too judgmental. You need to stop throwing the blame at each other and yelling. This only damages your relationship. It is best for you and your partner to sit down and speak. Make open communication a key element of your relationship. If you are single, you need to ensure that you are not hasty with your decisions. Take your time to determine if the person you are attracted to is the right one for you.

Profession

Regarding your career, this card indicates that you are constantly being evaluated or assessed. You may be in line for a promotion but would not know it. Always be careful about how you represent yourself. You are being watched.

Health

In terms of health, this card indicates that you will overcome an illness and feel whole soon. You have forged through difficult times, and your experiences will help you on the road to recovery.

Spirituality

This card indicates that you have learned everything you need to from your experiences in terms of your spirituality. You have identified the lessons that the universe wants to teach you and can now make enlightened decisions.

Reverse Position

Key Meanings

Unfair, false accusations, unwillingness to learn

General Interpretation

This card in the reversed position suggests that you are holding yourself back because of self-doubt and fear. Take action now. If you dilly-dally, you will lose the opportunities available to you. You also should not let people determine what you need to do in life.

Romance

If you are single, this card indicates that your embarrassment makes it hard for you to approach the person in whom you are interested. Never let your fear hold you back. Approach the person and know what he or she feels about you. If you are in a relationship, the card indicates that you and your partner are not willing to discuss matters that determine the relationship's status. Stop ignoring things. You need to know where the relationship is going and see if you and your partner are on the same page.

Profession

When this card appears in the reversed position, it indicates that you are at the turning point in your life. Your actions will make or break you. Do not be indecisive and seize every opportunity available to you.

Health

In terms of health, this card indicates that you need to let go of any negativity, especially if you suffer from an illness. Do not blame someone for causing you pain. When you hold onto negativity, you cannot recover easily. Accept your situation and let go of your past.

Spirituality

This card indicates that you are either refusing or ignoring your karmic lessons. The universe wants you to learn something, and if you ignore your lesson, the next lesson will be very difficult. You must give yourself enough time to learn so you can move ahead.

The World

Upright Position

Key Meanings

Fulfillment, success, travel

General Interpretation

This card signifies that you have the world at your feet. The card also indicates that new opportunities are opening up for you. You will also travel and be welcomed with open arms in other countries. Since you have worked hard to reach this level, go out there and celebrate.

Romance

If you are in a relationship, this card signifies that you have reached where you wanted to be. Maybe you wanted to be married or have children. You and your partner need to find a balance and make sure you are both on the same page. If you are single, this card signifies that you have many options available to you. Ensure that you are open to possibilities.

Profession

This card signifies that you will achieve all your goals. If you have set up your business, you will have reached your point of success. Now, enjoy the fruit of success.

Health

If this card arises in your reading, it means you need to overcome your health issues. This card is a great sign you will recover.

Spirituality

When this card appears in your reading, it indicates that you have learned what the universe is teaching you. You know who you are, what your path is, and how you fit into this world. You are in tune with your inner spirit, and your spiritual planes are opening up for you.

Reversed Position

Key Meanings

Disappointment, lack of completion

General Interpretation

This card indicates that you have achieved your goals, but now things have stagnated since you have nothing more to work towards. This means you need to throw your energy into learning something new or working on a new goal. Otherwise, you will be disappointed and feel like you are stuck.

Romance

If you are single, you need to go out and meet people. Do not let the feeling of loneliness creep in. You also cannot expect a person to come and knock on your door. If you are in a relationship, this card indicates that your relationship has stagnated. You and your partner both need to work on improving the relationship.

Profession

This card indicates that you have met all your goals. This signifies that you are not meeting your potential. Ask yourself if anything is holding you back or what you fear. You are the master of your life. Do not worry about making mistakes because that is how you learn.

Health

When this card is in the reversed position, it indicates that you need to revisit your treatment methods if you are suffering from an illness. If you are using the same treatments repeatedly, know that they do not work. Do not take shortcuts and work on the right methods to help you resolve your health.

Spirituality

This card represents the connection between you and your spirit. The reverse position indicates this connection is stagnant, and you need to find the will to progress. If so, you may need to try a different process. You cannot use shortcuts to learn more about your spirituality. You need to follow a path and try to learn more about your spirituality.

Chapter Seven: The Minor Arcana

The Minor Arcana may not be as important as the Major Arcana, but the cards do have some significance. The cards in the Minor Arcana tell you about the driving force of your life. It will indicate to you why you behave the way you do. It tells you about the concerns you may face in the future. There are 56 cards in this Arcana divided into four suits, just like the regular playing cards – Wands, Cups, Swords, and Pentacles.

Wands

The Wands is the suit that depicts creativity. The cards in this suit are associated with these qualities – self-esteem, self-confidence, enthusiasm, and creativity. They indicate to you your creativity.

Cups

This suit depicts your spirituality and emotional stability. When you pull cards from this suit during your reading, your interpretations of those cards help you better understand your emotions and feelings. You learn to understand what the higher power is saying to you and learn more about your feelings towards your partner.

Swords

The Swords depict your intelligence and way of thought. The cards in this suit help you understand your beliefs and morals. They indicate certain characteristics that help you understand your true self better.

Pentacles

This suit depicts all your concerns and fears, which could either be material or practical. They tell you what you most love doing and also whether you enjoy spending time with family and friends. The suit also indicates your perspective towards life.

Chapter Eight: Wands of Fire

This suit of cards is related to daily events, and they are connected to fire. When you work with wand cards, imagine you are working with fire. This means the cards you pick are volatile, full of energy, and temperamental. This suit is an indicator of your willpower. It is the source of all the energy in your reading. If a card from this suit appears in your reading, it represents your creativity and intelligence.

Upright Position

The suit of wands in the upright position indicates that you are a source of passion, inspiration, drive, and courage. The cards from this suit propel most actions you perform. You may also want to change aspects of your life using the energy from this suit. If the card is in the upright position during your reading, it indicates that you are an action-oriented, passionate, open, and adventurous individual.

Reversed Position

When the cards from this suit appear in the reversed position during a reading, it signifies weaknesses. The cards' energy in this suit is both powerful and destructive, and you should be careful when you use this energy. Fires provide warmth and light, but they can burn things to dust. This suit of cards is temperamental, and it moves from one end of the spectrum to the other in seconds. If this card appears in the reversed position, it indicates you are volatile and reckless.

The Cards

There are 14 cards, and the first card is the Ace of Wands. As you progress through the cards, you see that the cards in this suit are similar to a deck of playing cards. This means you have all the numbered cards as well as the four Court cards – the Knight, Page, King, and Queen.

Ace of Wands

If this card appears in your reading, be aware of a fateful or pivotal act you may perform, which will lead to a chain of events that will help you achieve your goal. This card refers to a new beginning or birth and the commitment you need to complete a project. It also indicates the beginning of a new journey. When this card appears in your tarot reading in the upright position, it means you should not take a bold step. If this card appears in the reversed position, it means you are not observing the signals and signs the higher power is sending you.

Two of Wands

This card is the second step of your journey. This is when you need to work on defining the plan to follow to achieve your goals. The plan you develop may need you to step out of your comfort zone. You learn to be more realistic and think about the long-term. This card in the upright position indicates you are making or will make the right decisions about life, while the reversed position indicates that you have created a deadlock for yourself because you are working with energies that cross each other. You may feel like you have taken up more than you can actually achieve. Always pay attention to how you feel about every decision you make. Do not jump the gun before you know what you want to do.

Three of Wands

When this card appears in your reading, it symbolizes a balance between your emotions and the journey you are taking. You will begin to feel more optimistic about your tasks and undertakings. When this card arises in the upright position in your reading, it indicates that you are someone who is adventurous and will do whatever it takes to meet their goals. You will be patient and learn to trust the right people. When it arises in the reversed position, it means you need to be confident and open about your ideas and learn to think big.

Four of Wands

This card indicates you should work with your team. It means you need to come together and create the right future for yourself. When this card appears in your reading, it indicates that you have the energy to begin your company. You need to work with others with the same energy as you to start the company. This is the only way you can create something positive to help you with the future. The card's upright position indicates you will start a new project or maybe get married. This card represents foundations. In the reversed position, this card indicates that you have forgotten to celebrate yourself. Therefore, it is time for you to celebrate every achievement you make along the way.

Five of Wands

This card represents the various struggles that one would face during their journey. In the upright position, the card indicates you demonstrate personal excellence, while in the reversed position, it indicates you are putting the people around you down to demonstrate this excellence. When this card appears in your reading, regardless of the position, ask yourself the following – who benefits when you fight hard to meet your goals? It is important to never let your ego guide you. If you do, you will always celebrate your successes alone.

Six of Wands

This card represents both recognition and respect for all the work and effort you are putting in to achieve your goals. The imagery on the card has a general who has led the troops to victory. This card often represents the victory parade. Since it took the entire army to achieve victory, but it was the general whose clarity and heroism led to victory. If this card appears in your reading in the upright position, it means you are doing well in your journey and will achieve success soon. If it appears in the reversed position, it means you need to trust yourself more and accept the praise and accolades people shower on you gracefully.

Seven of Wands

This card represents the people who can achieve their goals through willpower. This individual is accomplished in every way. If this card appears in the reversed position, it means you are letting your smugness and ego cloud your achievements. Your successes do not make you God, which means you can still make mistakes. When this card comes in the upright position, it indicates that you need to learn to stand up for yourself. Never let the fame get to your head. This will only make it harder for you to achieve your goals.

Eight of Wands

When this card appears in your reading, either in the upright or reversed position, it means the situation is escalating quickly. The appearance of this card indicates you need to accept change since it is necessary. You need to find the energy to keep up with this change. Understand that you cannot control things that happen in your life. If this card appears in the upright position, it means you need to find the energy to complete everything you have started now. Get busy and let your energy help you meet your goals. If it appears in the reversed position, it means you are wasting precious time.

Nine of Wands

When this wand appears in your reading, it means you need to rest for a bit. Give yourself enough time to restore energy, mend physical and mental wounds, and appreciate and enjoy your victories. There may be other obstacles that can arise during the process, but take a step back and assess the situation. It may be hard to do this, but trust that the people around you could take care of themselves and the project. If you make yourself irreplaceable, it means you do all the work yourself. If this card appears in your reading, it means you are considered irreplaceable, and this needs to change. If someone wants to help you, let them do it.

Ten of Wands

When this card appears in your reading, it indicates that you cannot rest and need to find a way to make it to the end. Otherwise, you are only letting yourself be vulnerable. Regardless of how difficult things may have become, do everything in your power to achieve your goals. When this card appears in your reading, it means you have taken up too much work to meet your goals. This card also represents the effort you need to make to complete the tasks in the queue.

Page of Wands

This card indicates you have a unique personality. You are independent and a nonconformist. You require nobody else's approval or affirmation when you want to do something. This card represents individuals who are rebels, innovators, or inventors. The card signifies freedom, and it holds a powerful message - one that says you have incredible power. It indicates you need to use the energy to achieve your goals. When this card appears in your reading in the upright position, it indicates you have a passion within you that will help you achieve your goals. It also indicates that it is time for you to explore and see what area of work interests you the most.

Knight of Wands

This card indicates you are a feisty and excited character. It also indicates you are easily provoked and are always ready to attack people who question you. You are filled with passion and energy and often fear no consequences. When this card shows up in your reading, it means your actions and attitude are intense. You must control your excitement and direct your energy in the right direction. You need to be intense in some situations, so *learn to control it.*

Queen of Wands

When this card appears in your reading, it indicates that you are a doer and leader. You will oversee the entire situation and ensure the team works well together. When this card appears in the upright position, it indicates that you are charming and charismatic. It also means you have infectious energy, which makes you lovable. In the reversed position, this card indicates that you need to be confident about what you do, learn to use your skills to lead your team with grace, and put yourself out there.

King of Wands

This card is a representation of the hero in you. Every individual is a mix of both feminine and masculine characters. When this card appears in your reading, it means you are an entrepreneurial, charismatic, and ambitious leader. This card means you never like sitting idly. You hate being bored and want to keep yourself busy. The card also means you want to lead a team and hate the idea of following another leader. You want to be loved and recognized by the people around you. The card indicates that you have immense energy and loves showering attention on the people he loves. You cannot control your emotions when someone crosses you. When this card appears in the reversed position, it indicates that you are too proud of yourself. It means you need to encourage the people around you and help them achieve success.

Chapter Nine: Swords of Air

This suit of cards is associated with change, conflict, and power. This suit of cards is associated with air, and if you see a card from this suit in your reading, it means you are looking for a solution to various external and internal struggles. These cards also mean it is time for you to make solid decisions. Let us now look at the different cards that make up this suit.

Ace of Swords

This is like the other ones or aces of any suit of cards. It indicates new beginnings. Since swords are often associated with discord, issues, and conflict, if this card shows up in your reading in the upright position, it indicates you have won. You may have struggled through the years to achieve your goals, but you are finally there because your hard work and zeal have paid off. If the card appears in the reversed position, it indicates that you are pushing yourself too hard. This means you need to calm down and relax. Let things take their course. If you keep working towards it without caring for anything around you, you will hurt somebody. The reverse position also indicates there are some people around you who are holding you back. Sit down and identify the problem.

Two of Swords

When this card appears in your reading, it indicates that you have trouble letting people in. If you build a wall around you, you can avoid being hurt by others, but it also prevents you from enjoying the great things destined for you. You should, therefore, spend some time to understand why you have your defenses up. Are you willing to let people in? If the card appears in the reversed position, it indicates that you are overprotective, either about others or yourself. This leads to some damage to the relationship. You must learn to be more open and let people do as they please. Give people some time before you judge them. You must understand the difference between stifling or suffocating the people you love and protecting them.

Three of Swords

It is unfortunate if this card comes up in your reading since it represents pain, heartache, and discontent, which are related to your relationships. Do you feel there is a love triangle? Do you find yourself feeling conflicted if you should be with another person? When this card appears in the upright position, it indicates you need to evaluate your relationships and make hard decisions to improve them. If the card appears in the reversed position, it means you can restore the relationship to its former level. All you must do is communicate, listen, and use your words carefully. This can help you and your partner overcome any silly issues that may have cropped up between the two of you.

Four of Swords

If you are feeling burned out or worn out, you are probably taking up more than you can chew. This card indicates that you need to step back and relax. Physical and emotional exhaustion could take a toll on you. You cannot function effectively if you do not give yourself enough time to recuperate. This does not mean you need to take a week off from work and spend it at the beach. The card only indicates that you need to spend enough time at home with family and friends to rejuvenate. You can also spend some time determining the things causing stress and finding a way to relieve yourself of it.

When this card appears in the reverse position, it indicates that you are someone who was plagued with fatigue and illness, but you are recovering from it. Having said that, your body can heal physically, but it takes some time for your brain to move on from the negativity and stress. This position also indicates that you need to get up and move. Move on from the ailments drowning you and focus on the future, not your past.

Five of Swords

When this card appears in your reading, it indicates that other people's actions hurt you. This means that you need to speak to the people around you who are causing you harm. It could also mean you are hurting somebody. Therefore, be strong enough to admit when you have hurt someone. The card can also indicate that people close to you may betray you. Therefore, ask yourself if you trust everybody around you. You must remember to ask the right questions to determine who can betray you. You must ensure that you ask these questions discreetly. When this card appears in the reverse position, it indicates that you are someone who cannot let go of any discussion or argument. This happens even if you have won that argument. You need to learn to let go, especially when people know your opinion. Once you have voiced your opinion, do not gloat or take pride in your actions. Move on.

The card also indicates that you may have some repressed resentment over a past or recent argument you had with a friend or family member. You may have had a heated discussion with them and still are upset with the outcome of the conversation. These repressed emotions will only damage you since you cannot develop harmonious relationships with the people around you.

Six of Swords

From what you have read so far, you know that swords symbolize turmoil and conflict, but they can have a positive result, as well. This is one such card since it indicates that your life will only improve now. You have braved through the storm, and things are now looking up for you. You are at that point in life where things are only going to get better for you. The card indicates you have grown up as a person and have learned to do better and effectively deal with your problems.

When this card appears in the reversed position, it indicates that your situation has not improved fully. It is on its way to getting better. The card is a sign you need to evaluate how you can improve your situation faster. Should you speak to someone? Is there some action you need to take such things to improve for you? When you have your answers, go out and get things done.

Seven of Swords

This card is an indicator you are being deceived. The card indicates there is someone in your circle not being honest with you. Ask yourself these questions if this card appears in your reading:

1. Can you trust everybody around you?
2. Do you know if someone is keeping secrets from you?

The person deceiving you does not have to only be a part of your personal life but can be from work. Determine if there is some colleague with whom you cannot connect. Ask yourself if the people at work comment about you behind closed doors. When this card appears in the reverse position, it indicates that you are often frustrated because you find you are left out. You tend to feel betrayed when the people around you do not let you in on their secrets. You need to understand that the people around you are not leaving you out of things because they do not want to tell you but are doing so because they did not think the matter was important.

Eight of Swords

Do you have trouble with meeting your deadlines and achieving your goals? This card indicates there is something holding you back from living up to your potential. You are worried about what people may say about you or worried about failure. If you do not want to try new things because you do not know how the situation will turn out, you need to stop doing that. This thought process will never get you anywhere. Be strong and take the risk. This card, in the reverse position, indicates you will move forward in life because you know how to deal with your insecurities and fears. And you no longer let your frustration show when people around you do not live up to your expectations. This is an asset, especially if you hold a leadership position.

Nine of Swords

This card is associated with depression, misery, anxiety, stress, and other mental illnesses in new age traditions. This card indicates that you are upset about things in life and have nobody around you to speak to about your pain. You need to pick up the phone and find someone who can help you overcome these issues. If you do not speak to someone, the illness and sadness will overwhelm you and ultimately consume you. It is easier to bear a burden if you share it with the people around you. When this card appears in the reversed position, it indicates that you need to communicate with the people around you. The card in the reversed position is a stronger indicator you need to meet with a professional to determine how you want to overcome your mental health issues. Find the right mental health professional to help you overcome your issues. This card is a sign you need to address your mental health issues on priority.

Ten of Swords

In most traditions, this card indicates that you are grieving. This can be due to a relationship ending, a loved one passing or anything important that has to end. This card is associated with sadness and heartache. In the reversed position, this card indicates that someone around you wants to cause you harm. This is when you need to look around you and determine if someone is trying to look for different means to harm you or make you suffer. Determine if someone gains from your suffering.

Page of Swords

This card is known as the messenger. When this card appears in your reading, it means you should look at your life and see what matters to you in life. Your excitement and enthusiasm will indicate to you this is the time to start anew. You can begin a new relationship or even your company. This card tells you that now is a good time to do this. If this card appears in the reversed position, it sends you the message you may not have good tidings in the days to come. You need to determine if there are people around you who behave in an impulsive, immature, and erratic way. If you know who these people are, you should avoid them at all costs. These people will bring you only down and make it harder for you to move forward. Maintain your distance from them since their habits and activities may draw you into their negative habits.

Knight of Swords

This card indicates you have someone who is determined, loyal, and has strong morals in your life. This person could be you or someone very close to you. This card signifies the individual and acts as a reminder you should always focus only on the truth. Do this even when you do not like what you see. When this card appears in the reverse position, it indicates that your excitement and enthusiasm can be detrimental to others. Do you think your excitement to do something new has made it difficult for your friends? Do you ignore them when you start something new? Did you stop thinking or caring for their needs? If you have done this as a mistake, then you should recognize what you have done and ask for forgiveness.

Queen of Swords

This card, like the other cards in this suit, can represent a concept or an individual. This is, however, dependent on the situation. In most readings, this card represents a stubborn and aloof woman who is respected and looked up to. Her attitude makes her less approachable. Other times, this card may represent the concept you are not letting people in because you believe you are better than the people around you. People may like you, but they may also fear you because you are not someone to whom they can speak. Learn to be open and respect people's views. When this card appears in the reverse position, it indicates that you are narrow-minded and judgmental. You do not want to listen to anything new or different because you are not willing to change the way you think. You like sticking to tradition. You are against change.

King of Swords

This card indicates that you are a person in a high position. You can claim your authority. This card also indicates that you are empowered and strong. The imagery on this card signifies fairness, honor, and truth. In some traditions, this card refers to a person in a position of authority. If this card appears in your reading, take a minute to think about how this card applies to you. When this card appears in the reverse position, it indicates that you are rigid and narrow-minded. The card also implies that you are very difficult to speak to, especially if someone wants to approach you with an idea different from yours. You may come across as judgmental or harsh because you cannot tolerate new concepts, ideas, or people.

Chapter Ten: Pentacles of Earth

This suit of cards is connected to the earth and is associated with various matters of wealth, security, and stability. Any card drawn from this is always drawn to the North. The cards in this suit relate to security, home, investments, wealth, money, job, and other matters that are associated with important aspects of life. These cards are similar to the Major Arcana cards and the suits we discussed above. There are different meanings to these cards if they are placed in the reverse position. This makes it important to understand how to interpret them.

This chapter will look at what each card indicates in their upright and reversed positions.

Ace of Pentacles

When this card appears in your reading, it indicates that abundance and prosperity are around the corner from you. Trust your intuition, and take the risk to make new beginnings. When this card is in the reversed position, it means you can expect a change in your finances. You may soon have trouble with your finances and have a feeling of emptiness. This card indicates you may hit rock bottom soon.

Two of Pentacles

When you draw this card in your reading, it indicates that you are playing around too much with your funds. You are probably borrowing from too many people and cannot repay them. The appearance of this card indicates that you will soon receive help. When this card appears in the reverse position, it means the situation is out of control. Therefore, you need to give yourself some space to change the way you act.

Three of Pentacles

This card indicates that you will soon receive rewards for all the work and tasks you have performed. You can expect an accolade or raise soon at work. When this card appears in the reverse position, it indicates that you will quarrel with your colleagues and family. This will only lead to frustration.

Four of Pentacles

This card indicates that you are stingy or thrifty. You are probably doing everything in your power to complete your tasks and work, but you are probably working too hard and being very careful about all the money you have earned. When the card is in the reverse position, it indicates that you are insecure and cautious about all your finances and never want to invest in risky investment options. You only behave this way because of your experiences. Do not, however, let this experience affect your judgment.

Five of Pentacles

This card indicates that you are on the verge of ruin or financial loss. This card may also indicate that you will have a loss when it comes to your spirituality. When this card appears in the reverse position, it indicates that you have already incurred a financial loss. This may leave you feeling helpless, and you can get past these feelings by working on improving things.

Six of Pentacles

When this card appears in your reading, it indicates that you love to give. You enjoy giving because you do it for the joy and not because it will help people around you to like or appreciate you. When the card is in the reverse position, it means there is a matter of security you need to concern yourself with. It also means you need to refrain from treating people unfairly.

Seven of Pentacles

When this card appears in your reading, it indicates that you enjoy working hard. The people around you recognize you for your efforts and appreciate your work ethic. When this card appears in the reverse position, it indicates that you should begin to save money. You need to do this to protect yourself from difficult situations. You should, however, not be stingy and reward yourself whenever you can.

Eight of Pentacles

This card indicates that you are finally doing what you love doing most. You also are extremely good at what you do. Since you know your talents, use them to your benefit. When this card appears in the reverse position, it indicates that you need to work on fine-tuning your skills. Work on your talents and turn them into an asset.

Nine of Pentacles

When this card appears in your reading, it indicates you are leading a good life and are secure. It also indicates that you are content with what you have. In the reversed position, this card indicates that you or someone around you uses ruthless and manipulation methods to get their way. This behavior only leads to trouble.

Ten of Pentacles

If you draw this card during your reading, it indicates that you will soon become wealthy. So, do not let any opportunities go by. In the reverse position, the card indicates disharmony in both your personal and professional life. You must learn to stop quarreling.

Page of Pentacles

When this card appears in your reading, it indicates that you will soon meet someone who loves life. This person will change the way you look at life. In the reverse position, this card indicates there is a lot of information or news coming your way about your job.

Knight of Pentacles

If you draw this card during your reading, it means you need to learn to share your fortune with the people around you. Learn to use your experiences to help the people around you succeed. The reversed position indicates that you always want to be the best at what you do. You do everything in your power to achieve your goals no matter what happens to the people around you. This means you will find yourself alone at the top.

Queen of Pentacles

If this card appears in your reading, it indicates that you are a productive and easy-going person. This card also indicates that you have an abundant life. In the reverse position, this card indicates that you try to overcompensate for feeling terrible by making more money.

King of Pentacles

When you draw the card during a reading, it indicates that you are a generous and kind individual. It also means you may need the help of a financial advisor. In the reversed position, the card indicates that you are very insecure about life and need someone to validate your every move.

Chapter Eleven: Cups of Water

This suit is related to the element of water and indicates feelings and emotions. The cards in this suit also indicate the relationships you share with the people in your life. If you pick many cups in your reading, it indicates that you are looking for some answers to your questions on family matters, love, and other relationships. Let us now look at each cup's meaning and how you can interpret them in the upright and reversed positions.

Ace of Cups

When this card appears in your reading, it indicates that you will have a new beginning. Since a cup is associated with abundance and relationships, this card indicates that you may fall in love soon. This love does not mean romantic love alone. It can imply new friendships and beginnings. This cup is associated with good fortune and spiritual insight and indicates that a miracle or blessing will soon occur. When the card appears in your reading in the reversed position, it indicates that you can expect sadness and disappointment soon. It may also indicate these feelings do not relate to you but relate to the people closest to you. The card can also indicate that you need to be wary of the feelings of the people around you. Think twice about what you want to say to them.

Two of Cups

When this card appears in your reading, it indicates that an existing relationship will develop soon. The card may also refer to an insignificant relationship in your life, indicating that you need to learn more about that person. Focus on your current relationships and find ways to enhance and strengthen them. In simple words, spend time with the people in your life and stop worrying about meeting new people. When this card appears in the reverse position, it indicates that you and your partner have had a disagreement. This is driving a wedge between the two of you, so you need to step back and reevaluate the situation. Try to be the bigger person and raise your peace flag.

Three of Cups

This card is often considered the party card. Since the imagery represents rejoicing and celebration, it can mean that a happy event is right around the corner. Do you know someone expecting their child or getting married? You can also think about your family and see how happy you are with the people around you. Ask yourself how you and your family connect. When the card appears in the reverse position, it indicates that disharmony and discord are around the corner. The people in your life are not malicious, but this situation arises only because of some conflicts you have. Leave your emotional baggage at home when you head out to meet your family. Your bad emotions and feelings cannot ruin your day.

Four of Cups

When this card appears in your reading, it indicates you need to understand if your relationship comes with conditions. It is important for you to discover what your partner expects from you in the relationship before you take it any further. Do you feel you are giving more than you get? Or vice versa? If yes, step back and evaluate your relationship. A relationship only functions if there is a balance between the individuals who are a part of the relationship. Ensure that the right people are in your life, and you like them. When the card appears in the reverse position, it indicates that your relationship is not as great as it seems. It may also have run its course. Sometimes, you may outgrow your relationship and find you and the other person have nothing in common. It could also mean the two of you no longer see eye to eye about certain issues. This means it is time for you to ask yourself the hard questions and determine if you need to break free of the relationship.

Five of Cups

When this card appears in your reading, it indicates that you are going through a rough patch. Since this cup is concerned with relationships, it indicates that you need to make some emotional sacrifices in your relationship. The card also indicates that you need to compromise and strike a balance with your partner. Compromise is not a negative thing. You may have to compromise a little to keep interesting pieces of information. The card can also indicate that you may be disillusioned or indecisive in the days to come, and this could happen if you are torn between two lovers. When this card appears in the reverse position, it indicates that you need to make a sacrifice soon. This time, the sacrifice is not an emotional one, which means you need to give up someone or something. You may not have been as attached as you believed, which makes it easier to let go.

Six of Cups

This card relates to all your memories. If this card appears in your reading, it suggests that some incidents and events in the past are significant and impact your present. These events may also affect your future. These events could be connected to your childhood or could have happened many years ago. The card shows that your past directly influences your present. It also indicates that you can expect some blessing from an admirer or friend. When this cup appears in the reversed position, it indicates that you need to be concerned about your recent memories. It also means a person with some influence over you is no longer a part of your life. That individual, however, still influences your decisions. This can either be good or bad, depending on the person's intentions. The card in the reversed position also indicates that you cannot let go of your emotions and baggage.

Seven of Cups

When this card appears in your reading, it indicates that you have many opportunities coming your way. You must, however, ensure that every decision you make is based on the larger picture. Stop focusing on what can help you in the short term. Do not be impulsive because that will not be beneficial to you. Always consider the long-term effect of every decision you make. What appeals to you now does not necessarily have to appeal to you in the future. This card may also refer to an individual using you for selfish reasons. When the card appears in the reversed position, it indicates that you are unhappy or bored at the moment. Since this is only a phase, be determined to give yourself some time. If you see an opportunity coming your way, grab it at the earliest and work on it.

Eight of Cups

Did you look at the waning moon in the imagery of the card? This image indicates that the relationship you did not give your full attention to is now ending. You need to accept that things have changed and move on. The card indicates that you will be disappointed in different aspects of your life. It can also indicate that you are seeking and wandering aimlessly. If this card appears in the reversed position, it indicates positivity. The card suggests that you need to reinvent and reevaluate yourself. You must learn to get rid of your old baggage and welcome new blessings and joys into life. This is the best way for you to move away from everything that has been holding you back. You must, however, be careful. Do not lose sight of your spiritual path.

Nine of Cups

When this card appears in your reading, it indicates that you finally have your wish. This card indicates both material success and emotional abundance. If you look at the card's imagery, it is a man who is happy and surrounded by cups. One assumption you can make is this individual is happy and has everything he needs around him. The card suggests that you have everything you want and are where you want to be. When the cup appears in the reverse position, it indicates that you have become complacent and have taken your relationships for granted. This will only lead to issues. Since the card also indicates abundance, it indicates that you are overindulging in pleasures when it appears in the reversed position. You must remember to stop wallowing in things that are great now because anything can change.

Ten of Cups

In most traditions, this card indicates happiness for the long-term. If this card appears in your reading, it indicates that your long-term relationships are growing and flourishing. You are finally at peace and content. In other cases, it may refer to a new beginning at home. This beginning could be anything from moving into a new home to getting married. If you look at the card's imagery, you can see a family looking at their house. This card only represents happiness and joy. In the reverse position, this card indicates issues at home. These issues will often sort themselves out, but you must be patient and compromise occasionally. The card also indicates that someone you trust may betray you.

Page of Cups

This card is like the other pages. It is known as a messenger card and means that the people around you are trying to grab your attention and want you to shower them with love and affection. This card may also indicate that you need to connect with people who are young and passionate. This individual is willing to do anything for you. In the reverse position, this card indicates someone who is moody and constantly wants your attention. This individual will do everything in his power to get you to notice them. If this card appears in the reverse position in your reading, it indicates that you may face obstacles and deception soon. It also indicates that someone doing something for you has an ulterior motive.

Knight of Cups

A cup card talks about relationships. This card indicates that you know how to stand their ground and stick to their morals. You, however, do not pick a fight with anybody over your morals and values. If this card does not refer to a person, it can refer to a new interest or passion. When this card appears in the reverse position, it indicates that you need to focus on people who want you to give them attention so they know they are doing well in life. There are some people in your life who want to be a part of your life for selfish reasons. Therefore, you need to watch out for deception and fraud. Stop committing to anything when it comes to the people around you.

Queen of Cups

This card, like all other cup court cards, represents a concept or person. This depends on the situation. In most readings, this card indicates that you are a sensual, understanding, and captivating individual. People around you are drawn to your charm since you are secure, honest, and loyal. If you are a woman, this card indicates that you are a great mother. The card indicates that you are someone who is kind and has a vision. When the card appears in a reverse position, it indicates that you are someone who is insecure. Sometimes, this card indicates that you are surrounded by people who are perverse and malicious. They use your insecurities and vulnerabilities to gain something from you.

King of Cups

When you draw this card during a reading, it indicates that you are someone who is ongoing and social. You are creative, entertaining, and outgoing. You also are skilled in numerous disciplines but are a master of more than one discipline. This is the card that most musicians, spiritual seekers, and artists want. When this card is in the reverse position, it indicates that you are a person with insecurities due to previous relationships. You are probably prone to depression. This person also has the authority and will do everything in their power to step over someone without thinking twice. You, however, need to be careful about these characteristics. You also need to ensure you never let people take advantage of you.

Chapter Twelve: Tips to Deepen Your Understanding of Tarot Symbolism

There are a lot of books and articles published over the years on Tarot reading. When you look at Tarot cards for the first time, you will feel overwhelmed. You may be very confused about whom you need to listen to and what interpretation you need to give your seeker. The truth is there is often no right answer.

There is a picture on every tarot card. These cards tell a story. You can use the story to help you connect with your subconscious mind. This interpretation is personal to you, and thus the interpretation varies from one person to the other. This book gives you the meaning behind the cards. You, however, need to practice before you begin Tarot reading.

When you work with these cards, you tend to develop an affinity towards some cards. If you use the technique detailed in the first chapter, you will connect with any card placed in front of you. These flashes of intuition leave you with a meaning that may contradict your previous understanding of the card. It is for this reason you need to choose a deck you connect with. This helps you develop your interpretations of the cards.

Once you choose a deck you connect with, it becomes easier for you to interpret the meaning. You can use the booklet to help you understand the meaning. Before you do this, place the cards in front of you and pick one. You can start with the Fool. Look very closely at the card, the colors, and the symbols on it. Try to determine what the picture means to you. Ask yourself these questions:

Does the card remind you of a certain event in your life, or does it remind you of a person? Do you relate to the situation in the picture? It is great if you do. You could then pick up another card and examine it as you did to the first. Then place that card next to the first card. Can you connect the two cards to each other? Is there a story? Continue to look at the cards. You will learn to build a story to help you answer different questions. See how things have changed from one point in the story to another.

Try to act like you are telling the story to someone. Look at the cards and use the image to help you come up with the story. Let your intuition control you. It may feel like imagination, but you are doing the best you can with your cards. This is the best way to connect to your subconscious and your intuition or your client to help you learn to read the Tarot cards.

When you read the cards for another person, you need to describe to them what is happening in the pictures. You will find yourself giving them an accurate reading. This will only come with time and practice.

When you have learned to read tarot cards, you will interpret the cards in front of you easily. You will learn to use stories to read the cards. Remember there is always a story you can read.

Conclusion

If you are a beginner, this book can act as your guide. It covers the information you need to know about tarot. It tells you how to interpret the meanings of the cards in the deck. There are different spreads that are used across the world. The book covers three spreads that are used often, and if you are a beginner, it is safe to use these spreads. This book also works as a refresher if you are an experienced tarot reader.

You are bound to make mistakes as a beginner but do not let this bring you down. If you are unsure or hesitant to perform a reading, do one for yourself. Practice as often as you can. You can use the meanings and interpretations in this book to help you develop the right interpretation.

The book takes you through each card in the major and minor arcana. It details the different ways these cards can be interpreted. When you begin with tarot reading, use these interpretations to help you. You will soon learn to interpret with ease. I hope the information in the book helps you with reading the cards well.

Here's another book by Mari Silva that you might like

PALM READING

Unlock the Secrets of Palmistry to Discover About You and Your Future

MARI SILVA

Your Free Gift (only available for a limited time)

Thanks for getting this book! If you want to learn more about various spirituality topics, then join Mari Silva's community and get a free guided meditation MP3 for awakening your third eye. This guided meditation mp3 is designed to open and strengthen ones third eye so you can experience a higher state of consciousness. Simply visit the link below the image to get started.

https://spiritualityspot.com/meditation

References

Chariot Tarot Card Meanings. (n.d.). Biddy Tarot website: https://www.biddytarot.com/tarot-card-meanings/major-arcana/chariot/

Payne-Towler, C. (n.d.). Tarot Suits: The Swords Cards. Tarot.com website: https://www.tarot.com/tarot/cards/suit-of-swords-meaning

Payne-Towler, C. (n.d.). Tarot Suits: The Wands Tarot Card Meanings. Tarot.com website: https://www.tarot.com/tarot/cards/suit-of-wands-meaning

Ranie, B. (2010, July 8). Tarot Card Meanings - The Star, the Moon, and the Sun. https://ezinearticles.com/?Tarot-Card-Meanings---The-Star,-the-Moon,-and-the-Sun&id=4627219

Suit of Pentacles Tarot Card Meanings. (n.d.). Biddy Tarot website: https://www.biddytarot.com/tarot-card-meanings/minor-arcana/suit-of-pentacles/

Suit of Wands Tarot Card Meanings. (n.d.). Biddy Tarot website: https://www.biddytarot.com/tarot-card-meanings/minor-arcana/suit-of-wands/

The Major Arcana Tarot Card Meanings. (2020, September 23). Tarot.com website: https://www.tarot.com/tarot/cards/major-arcana

The Major Arcana. (n.d.). thetarotguide website: https://www.thetarotguide.com/major-arcana

The Suit of Pentacles Tarot Card Meanings. (2020, January 28). Labyrinthos website: https://labyrinthos.co/blogs/tarot-card-meanings-list/the-suit-of-pentacles-tarot-card-meanings

The Suit of Wands Tarot Card Meanings. (2020, January 28). Labyrinthos website: https://labyrinthos.co/blogs/tarot-card-meanings-list/the-suit-of-wands-tarot-card-meanings

Wigington, P. Learn Religions website: https://www.learnreligions.com

Printed in Great Britain
by Amazon